THE
PROPER
BALANCE

THE PROPER BALANCE

A Practical Look at Liturgical Renewal

JOSEPH M. CHAMPLIN

Ave Maria Press
Notre Dame, Indiana

Nihil Obstat:

Rev. Richard Kopp
Censor Deputatus

Imprimatur:

Most Rev. Frank J. Harrison
Bishop of Syracuse
April 7, 1981

©1981 by Ave Maria Press, Notre Dame, Indiana 46556.

International Standard Book Number: 0-87793-233-6

Library of Congress Catalog Card Number: 81-68000

Printed and bound in the United States of America.

Text design: Elizabeth French
Cover design: Carol A. Robak

*For Monsignor Martin B. Hellriegel
and other pioneers like him
who loved the liturgy long before
the last decade and whose impact
on our liturgies will extend
far beyond the next one.*

Contents

Foreword

It is almost 20 years since the Fathers of the Second Vatican Council debated the proposed Constitution on the Liturgy. It is more than a decade since the publication of Pope Paul's revision of the Order of Mass. It is certainly time to review successes and failures, strengths and weaknesses, as the church community, God's people, celebrates the mysteries of the Eucharist and the other sacraments.

This book will be a major help in the review and in the catching up with what has been done in the reform. The catching up, almost everyone will agree, is necessary.

Before the Second Vatican Council, it used to be said that liturgical renewal, though soundly conceived, had touched only the tiniest fraction of the church's people and their ministers. Since then, everyone has been touched by liturgical reform or revision, but not always by liturgical renewal.

This extremely useful book has two parts. The first might be called the assessment: how far and how well we have traveled the road of change. The author gives a balanced treatment, avoiding the extremes of dissatisfaction—on the right, a small and strident minority not yet reconciled to the conciliar decisions and the papal revision; on the left, a small, less strident, but sometimes equally arrogant minority unwilling to pay the price of the gradual development that is demanded to preserve the communion of the churches of God.

Of greater importance, especially for catching up, is the review of what has been done by the official revisers of the Roman liturgy of the Mass—and now, as the Council explicitly planned, what is open to regional and cultural adaptation of liturgical forms. This makes up the second part of the book.

Perhaps this review of texts and directives, descriptive of the style of celebrating Mass, should be compared—favorably—with the work of modern, preconciliar rubricians. The latter failed because of their excessive precision and rigidity and above all by the absence—there were exceptions—of rationale for rites and forms. The present treatment is at once informational and motivating. It is informational because it provides what many presiding celebrants and their planning committees often lack: a clear picture of the rite as officially set down, happily with all kinds of accommodations, choices and flexibility. It is motivating because, like the revised liturgical books of Pope Paul VI and the ancillary liturgical instructions of the postconciliar period, it offers the underlying sense of liturgical rite so lacking in the past.

One can think of many audiences and many uses for this commentary. Ministers and all who have a special role in preparing and celebrating Mass surely need much more than an amateur knowledge of the rite. Each element or dimension of the celebration, even the smallest ritual action, has or should have its value in the total eucharistic sign. This book provides a valuable introduction to the directions and explanations of the sacramentary and fleshes out some of its content. It should move the reader to a thorough study of all the introductory front matter of the sacramentary, including such significant documents as the *Directory for Masses with Children* and the profound apostolic letter of Paul VI on the church year.

In the April 14, 1940, issue of *Worship* (then called *Orate, Fratres*), there is a visionary and prophetic article by H. A. Reinhold, "My Dream Mass." The lively writer describes an ideal parochial celebration of the Eucharist, but with several disclaimers lest he appear to be a radical reformer. In effect what he described in 1940 was the revised Order of Mass of the Second Vatican Council and Pope Paul. Thus not merely two decades but four decades have gone by since the ritual revision was opened up for study and discussion. Perhaps this suggests that no passage of time alone can create a living and effective liturgical celebration, but only continued and renewed reflection upon the liturgy, its style and significance.

This book is welcome as a needed aid to reflection and action.

Rev. Frederick R. McManus
Vice Provost and
Dean of Graduate Studies
Catholic University of America;
former *Director, Secretariat,*
Bishops' Committee on the Liturgy

Author's Preface

After Jesus' disciples had been active in the ministry for a period of time, they returned and reported to the Lord "all that they had done and what they had taught."

Their master then responded: "Come by yourselves to an out-of-the-way place and rest a little" (Mark 6:31).

By this advice, Christ in effect was stressing to his first and later laborers the need for prayer and reflection in the midst of an active apostolate.

We seem today to be at a similar juncture in our liturgical ministry, requiring a resting place where those involved can review what they have done and taught. During the past decade priests, deacons, worship leaders and community members have received officially revised ritual books, studied those texts, introduced these rites on the parish level and celebrated them.

Now we might take time to pause a little, reflect on that experience and draw out some conclusions for our liturgies in the decade ahead.

This book has been designed to help with such a process.

Part I examines the past and the future from a broad, general perspective, although with numerous specific illustrations. It looks at progress made, mentions pitfalls which developed and offers projections for the eighties.

Part II examines the Mass part by part and step by step in some detail. It compares what the church desires and directs in eucharistic celebrations with what sometimes has actually been happening.

Celebrants, liturgical ministers and worship committees will, we hope, find the material in Part II a kind of check list or examination of conscience. A comparison between current practice and authoritative rubrics should confirm good habits and reveal poor ones. With those insights we can move forward during the next decade celebrating worship with that delicate, correct, proper sense of balance needed for liturgy which gives suitable praise to the Lord and touches the hearts of God's people.

I wish to extend my gratitude to Father Frederick McManus, one of those liturgical pioneers noted in the dedication, for his suggestions, his foreword to this book and his invitation back in 1968 to labor in Washington with him at the Liturgy Secretariat for the Bishops' Committee on the Liturgy.

I also offer my appreciation to Mrs. Patricia Gale of Camillus, New York, who accurately, efficiently and graciously typed the manuscript.

Part I
The Past and Future Decades

Chapter One:
Ten Years of Progress

Just one decade ago, my book *Christ Present and Yet to Come* was published. It carried the subtitle "The Priest and God's People at Prayer," and appeared at the same time as the new Roman Missal and other liturgical books. The book sought to provide some practical guidelines for priests, especially in their role as celebrants of revised Catholic worship services.[1]

Those were days of frequent and radical changes both inside and outside the church. Priests felt, like everyone else, the unsettling effect of a period during which many traditional attitudes and methods of doing things simply fell by the wayside. When those changes began to touch formerly frozen liturgical rites, an enormous challenge loomed for a clergy trained in a totally different approach. The liturgy became more flexible and this flexibility caused tensions among the people in the pews as well as in the priest at the altar.

Four hundred years earlier, in 1570, Pope Pius V issued a Roman Missal, the fruit of the Council at Trent, which brought together widely diverse liturgical practices and gave the Mass both a needed unity as well as a strong uniformity. Shortly thereafter, in 1588, Pope Sixtus V established the Sacred Congregation of Rites, a Vatican office designed to resolve difficulties about the missal, give interpretations and make specific rulings on worship matters.

Over the next centuries, the Roman liturgy maintained a stable, monolithic structure. Those who lived at least some of their adult Catholic life in pre-Second Vatican Council days recall easily that form of worship.

"Mass is always the same wherever you go throughout the whole world" we would tell inquiring friends or those interested in entering the church. Ceremonies for baptisms, weddings and funerals varied hardly at all except for slightly different music on some occasions. A congregation could recognize the Sunday scripture texts almost as soon as the priest (who read both biblical passages) began the initial verse since the identical ones returned year after year. The clergy followed precise, detailed instructions or rubrics when they "said" Mass or "administered" the sacraments.

Official liturgical reform actually began at the turn of our century and continued with occasional, specific revisions prior to the Second

Vatican Council. It reached a comprehensive, fulfilled stage at the start of the last decade, shattering the quality of stonelike sameness.

First of all, the *Constitution on the Sacred Liturgy* insisted that participation by the people must be central both in the reform of the worship rites and in their implementation on the practical level.

> By way of promoting active participation, the people should be encouraged to take part by means of acclamations, responses, psalmody, antiphons, and songs, as well as by actions, gestures and bodily attitudes. And at the proper times all should observe a reverent silence.[2]

Secondly, the renewed liturgical books were to offer a rich variety of readings, prayers and other options from which the priest and members of the congregation should select those most appropriate for the particular celebration.

This truly was flexibility, not only sanctioned, but encouraged by the church. For example, in article 313, the General Instruction of the Roman Missal described just how a worshiping community, including the celebrant, ought to use these abundant resources incorporated within the authorized volumes.

> The pastoral effectiveness of a celebration depends in great measure on choosing readings, prayers, and songs which correspond to the needs, spiritual preparation, and attitude of the participants. This will be achieved by an intelligent use of the options which are described below.

21

> In planning the celebration, the priest should
> consider the spiritual good of the assembly rather
> than his own desires. The choice of texts is to be
> made in consultation with the ministers and
> others who have a function in the celebration, in-
> cluding the faithful.[3]

Finally, the church set before priest celebrants a fresh and challenging ideal. The reformed rubrics no longer minutely regulated their gestures and words, but provided them with opportunity for a more natural, comfortable, personal and creative style of celebration. They still maintained, however, definite guidelines for the preservation of order, tradition and unity in the liturgy. Moreover, the priest now had the responsibility of involving the congregation in planning and executing a celebration.

In addition, the council fathers reminded the clergy: "Pastors of souls must therefore realize that, when the liturgy is celebrated, more is required than the mere observance of the laws governing valid and licit celebrations."[4]

From a theological and theoretical perspective, liturgical specialists like Benedictine Father Kevin Seasoltz saw the need for a different attitude within the priest as he approached the liturgy. *Christ Present and Yet to Come,* written from a more pastoral viewpoint, reflected the judgment of such scholars, and focused on the priest as "Shepherd, Preacher, Celebrant," "Leader of Christian Worship," and "President of the Community." Other sections dealt with being relaxed and natural, having a healthy regard for rubrics, planning the liturgy and communicating through reading, preaching and proclaiming. There was, then, an anxiety about the new liturgy and yet an eagerness to learn how to say Mass all over again. Sales of the book, now out of print, indicate that half the priests in the U.S. purchased it and presumably at least looked it over.

Today we possess a decade of experience with the new liturgical books, the more flexible form of Catholic worship and the new style of priest celebrants. What are the results, the plus and minus effects, the positive fruits and the harmful faults of those renewal efforts?

On April 17, 1980, Pope John Paul II offered the *Norms on Eucharistic Practices* through an instruction on "the priceless gift of the Holy Eucharist" issued by his Sacred Congregation for the Sacraments and Divine Worship. At the outset, the Holy Father and his Vatican office noted "with great joy the many positive results of the liturgical reform."[5]

I would like to list the particular benefits cited by this document, as well as offer some examples and comments.

1) "A more active and conscious participation by the faithful in the liturgical mysteries."

An hour ago we completed our annual Thanksgiving Day Mass at St. Joseph's parish in Camillus, New York. The very fact that 750 people came to church to begin the holiday festivities with a liturgy giving thanks to the Lord

represents a drastic change and vast improve-
ment over recollections of what happened in
my childhood and early days as a priest. Some
people can recall when Catholics considered
Thanksgiving a "Protestant feast" and thus one
they avoided or limited to enjoying a turkey
dinner.

Like so many other American parishes, this
church has discovered the beauty of fully participating in a special Thanksgiving Eucharist.
Consider a few of its elements, things hardly
dreamed possible a decade or two ago: beautiful
vernacular texts for the Mass, approved by the
U.S. bishops; the congregation speaking
responses to invitations from the celebrant; the
community singing several hymns, acclamations
like "Holy, holy, holy Lord," and the "Our Father";
the resident priests concelebrating the Mass and
joined by a priest from the parish home for the
holiday to visit his parents; every participant
coming forward at the presentation of gifts with
an item of food for the poor (over $1000 in canned
foods amassed before the altar forms a magnificent picture and raises people's awareness of the
needy); a family, later, bringing the bread and
wine to the sanctuary for the liturgy of the
Eucharist; the sign of peace joyfully extended
around the church; communion under both kinds
available for those who so choose; the consecrated bread received either on the tongue or in
the hand according to the communicant's
preference; lay persons assisting the clergy with
distribution of the Eucharist; the priests

standing at each entrance afterwards exchanging holiday wishes with parishioners.

This one celebration alone exemplifies the profound shift in our style of worship as well as the positive result – more active and conscious participation by the faithful in the liturgy.

2) "Doctrinal and catechetical enrichment through the use of the vernacular and the wealth of readings from the Bible."

During my first years as a priest I distributed ashes, blessed throats, gave communion, anointed bodies, witnessed marriages and baptized babies in Latin. That language had a sense of awesomeness, mystery and universality to it, but hardly ever did a person understand the content of those words.

Today the priest says "Remember that you are dust . . ." instead of "Memento, homo, quia pulvis . . ."; he recites prayers at those sacramental liturgies in the vernacular which have a richness of meaning and the power to touch; he shows the host to individuals and offers them invitations to express their faith with the words, "The Body of Christ."

The majesty of Latin may have disappeared, and that is a loss, but the teaching opportunities which accompany introduction of English within the liturgy are enormous.

Prior to the Second Vatican Council, Catholics were simply not biblically oriented people. Some of our liturgies contained a few scriptural passages, but those used were limited in number and repetitious. We read the same texts on Sundays every year and had no assigned passages for weekdays.

The council fathers directed: "In sacred celebrations a more ample, more varied and more suitable reading from sacred scripture should be restored."[6] They also decreed: "The treasures of the Bible are to be opened up more lavishly so that a richer fare may be provided for the faithful at the table of God's word. In this way a more representative part of the sacred scriptures will be read to the people in the course of a prescribed number of years."[7]

Our lectionary of readings for Sundays, weekdays and other celebrations may well be one of the more productive fruits of the current worship reform. The ideal of the church today is that no liturgical service be without some excerpt from the inspired word. The three-year Sunday and two-year weekday cycles of texts have indeed provided a richer fare of biblical food for Roman Catholics. In fact, our liturgies on weekends currently contain, quantitively, more scriptural passages than most Protestant churches.

3) "A growth in the community sense of liturgical life."

The two thousand bishops at Vatican II agreed to this principle: "It must be emphasized that rites which are meant to be celebrated in common, with the faithful present and actively participating, should as far as possible be celebrated in that way rather than by an individual and quasi-privately."[8]

When Jean Lehman faced serious surgery for the removal of a diseased intestine, Father Thomas McKeon, the hospital chaplain, helped her prepare for the operation by ministering the sacrament of the anointing of the sick. Her entire family plus a few close friends participated and, at the end, all sang a hymn which echoed down the corridors of the secular medical center.

This type of community celebration has become a regular event for Catholics today. To cite a few other examples: common penance services at Christmas, Lent and for first penance; a joint anointing service once a year in church; baptisms within Sunday Mass; official greeters at weekend liturgies welcoming newcomers; eucharistic ministers carrying the Lord each Sunday to house-bound parishioners; adults joining the church on Holy Saturday night during the Easter vigil.

The growth in our awareness of the liturgy's communal dimensions spoken of by Pope John Paul II becomes more evident as one reflects for a moment on what has happened in the seventies.

4) "Successful efforts to close the gap between life and worship, between liturgical piety and personal piety and between liturgy and popular piety."

In 1965, the bishops gathered at Rome wrote, "The joy and hope, the grief and anguish of the men of our time, especially of those who are poor or afflicted in any way, are the joy and hope, the grief and anguish of the followers of Christ as well. Nothing that is genuinely human fails to find an echo in their hearts."[9]

Since the liturgy expresses the life of the church, this explicit desire of the Council to embrace all of the needs and experiences of contemporary humankind would naturally affect the tone of Catholic worship in the years which followed.

The restoration of the ancient common prayer or prayer of the faithful at all Sunday Masses illustrates one of the steps in response to that desire. Now we employ this more structured, varied and extensive format rather than reading a list of sick and deceased persons, or mentioning a critical intention at announcement time, and saying an Our Father or Hail Mary for them.

In the words of the Roman Missal, which in turn took its direction from the *Constitution on the Sacred Liturgy*: "It is appropriate that this prayer be included in all Masses celebrated with a congregation, so that intercessions may be made for the Church, for civil authorities, for those oppressed by various needs, for all mankind, and for the salvation of the world."[10]

Commercial publications containing such intercessions or parish committees designed to compose them seek to fulfill that function of bringing the world outside into the worship inside our churches, of fusing liturgy and life.

The sacramentary and lectionary contain many prayer formulas and scriptural texts for special needs. Along with greater freedom within the church calendar and the liturgy's structure itself these better enable celebrants, worship committees and communities to match a celebration with current needs.

When 75 people crowded the chapel at Holy Family parish in Fulton, New York, one fall afternoon to participate in the regular weekday Mass, they had a special purpose in mind. Fran Tetro and his two hunting companions had been missing for ten days, their downed private aircraft sighted, but their fate not yet determined. These relatives and friends joined his wife Dorothy and three young children to pray for deliverance, understanding and courage. The official books provided exceptionally touching and pertinent words to fit this tense and anxious situation.

The *Constitution on the Sacred Liturgy,* in article 13, highly recommends popular devotions of the Christian people, provided they conform to church laws and norms.

Those devotions "should be so drawn up that they harmonize with the liturgical seasons, accord with the sacred liturgy, are in some way derived from it, and lead the people to it, since in fact the liturgy by its very nature is far superior to any of them."

New Vatican norms for exposition of the Blessed Sacrament and devotional services which involve the Eucharist are gently, gradually bringing Catholics to this better perspective about the liturgy and private or personal prayer. For instance, congregational song, scriptural proclamations and various prayers must always accompany benediction. Moreover, the same number of candles for Mass as for benediction, and the same, single genuflection instead of a both knee reverence before the exposed sacrament, silently speak of the correct relationship between Mass and the reserved Eucharist.

Those who have worked to implement the liturgical reforms approved by the church know well how painful these changes have been for some priests and parishioners. How many or what percentage opposed the revisions in the beginning is not clear, but we do possess scientific data that now the vast majority of Catholics have come to understand and accept the renewed rites.

Liturgist John Gallen, S.J., in a recent article, "Reforming the Liturgy, Again" writes: "In the United States, according to a statistical analysis sponsored by the Federation of Diocesan Liturgical Commissions and conducted by the National Opinion Research Center of the University of Chicago, more than 80 per cent of American Catholics favor the reform."[11]

There have been, then, many positive results of the liturgical reform. Can we also note any negative effects which developed during the past decade and continue with us today? The next chapter will examine that issue.

Chapter Two:

A Little Too Far and Too Fast?

It is unwise to judge past events solely by present conditions. Developments, particularly unhealthy ones, which arose a quarter of a century ago, grew out of a particular set of circumstances that no longer exist. To understand those movements or directions in perspective, then, we must look back at that time and climate which dominated the country and church. Our modern liturgical reforms should be reviewed by this same process.

The major official and unofficial ritual changes in Catholic worship began soon after World War II, with the heaviest concentration of them during the sizzling sixties. During that turbulent decade changes of all sorts were in the air. Protest, rejection of authority, clamor for freedom, anti-establishment slogans, all dominated both secular and religious life. That naturally affected priests as celebrants and all those vitally concerned about pastoral life and the liturgy. They were both infected by the atmosphere around them and anxious to adapt the church's public prayer to such rapidly shifting demands.

In the face of this demand for change stood ritual books largely unchanged for 400 years, and church regulations which insisted that only the Vatican or the bishop may make adjustments in the liturgy. For example, prior to the Second Vatican Council, only the Holy See had the right to alter the church's official worship. After Vatican II, that power was extended somewhat to the bishops and to the bishops' conferences of a country. Still the *Constitution on the Sacred Liturgy* insisted that "Therefore, no other person, not even a priest, may add, remove, or change anything in the liturgy on his own authority."[1]

Even normally very obedient and respectful priests felt deep frustration as they witnessed the needs of their people and judged that the older books or rules were obstacles keeping them from responding to those spiritual concerns.

I have a clear picture in my own mind of an interfaith wedding at which I presided in the early sixties. One spouse was half Jewish and her father, remarkably and with great pain, came to the service, the first time he had ever stepped inside a Christian church. In those days we celebrated part of the ritual in the vernacular, the rest in Latin, including a beautiful Hebrew-based blessing. With great daring I transgressed the law and on the spot translated "Deus Abraham, Deus Isaac, Deus Jacob sit vobiscum . . ." into "May the God of Abraham, the God of Isaac and the God of Jacob be with you. . . ."

The joy and comfort which I saw on the faces of the Jewish guests as they heard those familiar words eased my uneasiness over having violated the strict rubrics. Those who, caught in similar conflicts between liturgical law and pastoral needs, went much faster and farther than I did, may chuckle at this minor illicit adaptation. But it does exemplify the struggles which dominated the scene at that time.

Church authorities were not oblivious to these conditions nor insensitive to the people's needs and the liturgy's inadequacies. The council fathers decreed:

> Holy Mother Church desires to undertake with great care a general restoration of the liturgy itself. For the liturgy is made up of unchangeable elements divinely instituted, and of elements subject to change. These latter not only may be changed but ought to be changed with the passage of time, if they have suffered from the intrusion of anything out of harmony with the inner nature of the liturgy or have become less suitable.[2]

However, the church responds in terms of centuries, not decades, and will not be pushed into hasty decisions which later prove premature. This restoration "with great care" would require that "a careful investigation — theological, historical, and pastoral – should always be made into each part of the liturgy which is to be revised. Furthermore the general laws governing the structure and meaning of the liturgy must be studied in conjunction with the experience derived from recent liturgical reforms and from the indults granted to various places."[3]

Such care, investigation, study and evaluation took time, too much time for many who could not wait for official adaptations and went off on their own. Some of those personal, private, grassroots efforts to update the liturgy were really excellent; others were horrendous. Some reflected a sound grasp of good worship; others seemed to emerge more out of a quest for novelty or an urgent wish to be relevant. Whatever their merits or limitations, these innovations widened and deepened the gap between authorized liturgy and pastoral practice. Those were days of great tension between universal or diocesan authority and local liturgical leadership.

During the late sixties and seventies, the fruit of official research began to appear in the revised liturgical books. Those texts, with their rich resources, encouragement for participation, and openness to creativity rather swiftly healed many wounds, diffused much tension and largely closed the chasm between official and unofficial worship.

Many of the valuable but unauthorized developments worked their way into the approved liturgy; most of the unsound, private innovations died and were discarded. Priests, deacons and pastoral liturgists worked hard to introduce and implement the revised rites, usually achieving very positive results although often encountering some opposition in the early stages.

Nevertheless, in such a period of flux we can still expect some creative efforts to move excessively in one direction or the other. Pope John Paul II has been aware of those tendencies and, in the instruction on *Norms on Eucharistic Practices,* could not "suppress concern at the varied and frequent abuses being reported from different parts of the Catholic world."[4] I would like to cite those mentioned in the decree and offer a few comments and applications.

1) "The confusion of roles, especially regarding the priestly ministry and the role of the laity."

This document offers, in a parenthesis, three examples of that misdirection: indiscriminate shared recitation of the eucharistic prayer, homilies given by lay people and lay people distributing communion while the priests refrain from doing so.

In the initial years of the total vernacular liturgy, some priests encouraged the congregation to join in with them as they recited the eucharistic prayer. It seemed from the beginning a well-intentioned, but ill-advised move.

Aside from the fact that the rubrics or church regulations specified otherwise, there were deeper, negative considerations about the practice. First of all, it eliminated or at least badly weakened the position of the priest as celebrant, leader of worship, or president of the community.

Secondly, it fostered a false notion that the only type of congregational participation was through a spoken or sung response, forgetting this critical remark from the *Constitution on the Sacred Liturgy* that "at the proper time a reverent silence should be observed."[5] Thirdly, it destroyed the dialogue notion of the eucharistic prayer by which the priest proclaims and the congregation responds.

From my experience across the country, I would judge that this development faded, for the most part, shortly after it began. I have heard of few places lately where the community joins with the celebrant for the entire eucharistic prayer. However, a joint recitation of the "Through him, with him, in him . . ." has become quite common, a procedure that effectively cancels the recitation of the great Amen by the congregation. The great Amen is either swallowed up and lost, or its character as a response destroyed.

The document deals precisely with this point: "The *Per Ipsum* itself is reserved to the priest. This Amen especially should be emphasized by being sung, since it is the most important in the whole Mass."[6]

The practice of persons other than priests or deacons preaching the homily has arisen, among other situations, in parishes where sisters or lay individuals serve as full-time pastoral associates.

In the United States, the use of religious and lay persons as eucharistic ministers has spread widely and rapidly with many magnificent spiritual results both for the designated distributors and the people they serve. They are meant, however, to assist, not replace the priests. The Vatican text thus declares: "A reprehensible attitude is shown by those priests who, though present at the celebration, refrain from distributing communion and leave this task to the laity."[7]

2) **"An increasing loss of the sense of the sacred."**

The instruction, again in a parenthesis, provides examples of this harmful trend: "Abandonment of liturgical vestments, the eucharist celebrated outside church without real need, lack of reverence and respect for the blessed sacrament, etc."[8]

Commonweal magazine has never possessed a reputation for being right-wing, conservative or opposed to change. In fact, I would judge the publication prides itself as a vehicle for the expression of "liberal" Catholic thinking. Those are all, of course, undefined labels and unhealthy stereotypes which we might better avoid using. My point, here, however, is to establish the background or climate of this periodical that carried a recent article, "Eggheads, Pumpkin Heads and Liturgical Popularism."

The author was a Dominican priest, David K. O'Rourke, pastor of St. Mary Magdalen's Church and professor of pastoral theology at the Graduate Theological Union in Berkeley, California. I do not know Father O'Rourke; I do know the G.T.U. at Berkeley would not be considered the national headquarters for a movement which seeks a return to the past or a tightening of church regulations.

In such a context, his observations have all the more impact:

> Today we celebrate liturgies that have lost a sense of the transcendent. As a result we have people looking . . . for a priest with power. Hand-wringing or mourning the past, or even trying to recapture the past, are all efforts to no good purpose. More to the purpose is a conscious and definite effort to rework the liturgy so that it be transcendent, an effort to use symbols that function in a transcendent way.[9]

We could safely replace "transcendent" with "sacred" in this quotation and see specific reinforcement for the assertion made by the Roman document.

John Garvey graduated from Notre Dame in 1967 and is a regular columnist for *Commonweal.* He shares some of the identical difficulties with Father O'Rourke and expressed them in his alma mater's alumni journal through an article entitled, "Somebody Stole the Mass."

> I am not nostalgic for the old forms. I think Mass in the vernacular is better than Mass in Latin, at least in theory, and the new liturgical cycle is richer in scripture than the old.
>
> However something has happened in the transition from old to new that is not entirely good. Now may be the time to figure out what went

wrong, because there probably will never be another generation with our peculiar experience of two very different liturgical worlds.[10]

It seems clear that the instruction views these abuses as a symptom, perhaps even a part of the cause for "what went wrong," this loss of the transcendent in worship.

3) "Misunderstanding of the ecclesial character of the liturgy."

The instruction, once more in a parenthesis, offers illustrations of the erroneous trend: "the use of private texts, the proliferation of unapproved eucharistic prayers, the manipulation of the liturgical texts for social and political ends."[11]

Once a month I spend several hours with a dozen outstanding young men, novices preparing for a life of teaching as Christian Brothers. All have college degrees, some even graduate degrees, but none with any serious training in liturgical theory or practice.

Recently our class evolved into a lively, even hotly debated discussion about making unauthorized changes in the Mass. The novices argued among themselves for and against. Their enthusiasm pleased me since it proved they had at least not fallen mentally asleep during the presentation.

One young man, however, truly warmed my heart. In earlier sessions, both his inquiries and own admission revealed a real absence of much understanding about the true nature of liturgy. Through these few meetings, nevertheless, he has come to grasp the wider, universal dimensions of Catholic worship. In his words, the Eucharist is not exclusively "my" nor even "our" (the local community's) Mass, but the liturgy of the whole church.

That expanding vision has had very practical consequences for him. He is a baker and previously enjoyed making the large loaves for Mass which were popular in some places prior to the recent instruction. Its restrictions about unleavened altar breads or loaves with ingredients over and above wheaten flour and water disappointed the novice, but he now judges those regulations, and others like the examples we have quoted from the norms, in a different perspective. The ecclesial character of the liturgy has become much clearer to him.

John Garvey rather sharply describes some particular developments in contemporary liturgies which bother him. His acid remarks lend support to the instruction's concern over the manipulation of liturgical texts:

> The belief that the celebrant of the Mass is a charismatic figure whose mood and personality should be expressed during the liturgy is all around us, like a seasonal virus. It is a clerical disease, but the laity suffer its consequences.
>
> I have been to an antiwar Mass at which communion was distributed with what looked like a lateral pass and children's Mass where they got everything down to where five-year-olds could understand.

I have a low threshold of cute. I find too much liturgical relevance (to either the political or the educational needs of the moment) hard to take.[12]

The instruction on the *Norms on Eucharistic Practice* concludes with these admonitions from previous decrees which warn about taking inappropriate liberties with the liturgy:

The Second Vatican Council's admonition in this regard must be remembered: "No person, even if he be a priest, may add, remove or change anything in the liturgy on his own authority." And Paul VI of venerable memory stated that, "Anyone who takes advantage of the reform to indulge in arbitrary experiments is wasting energy and offending the ecclesial sense.[13]

If private liturgical reforms may have gone a bit too far during the last decade or so, there are some who would argue they also went a bit too fast.

At the question period after a lecture in Silver Spring, Maryland, one man made this point quite well. He compared the introduction of an entirely new Order of Mass with the Esso Corporation's shift in its name. Most parishes, in his opinion, spent one, two or a few sermons on the topic, then expected everyone to adjust and accept immediately, without complaint, the revised rite. Esso, on the other hand, carefully planned, took a long period of time for implementation and spent millions of dollars for the simple change in its title to Exxon.

As one who gave a substantial portion of his

last 20 years to writing and speaking about changes in the church I must agree with the man. Especially during the early set of worship reforms, we neglected to give sufficient attention to the emotional and psychological dimensions of the change process. There was no malice involved, but we had neither the structural setup for a comprehensive program of initiating new rituals nor did we possess the awareness of just how complex are the reactions of people when something novel enters their lives. Moreover, we relied too much on the printed word, not realizing that the elaborate explanations of the rites and changes that appeared in official books and sources would never reach a mass audience.

Alvin Toffler in his book, *Future Shock,* provides a very helpful insight about this intricate and volatile issue. He wrote:

> Almost invariably, research into the effects of change concentrate on the *destinations* toward which change carries us, rather than the *speed* of the journey. In this book, I try to show that the rate of change has implications quite apart from, and sometimes more important than, the directions of change. No attempt to understand adaptivity can succeed until this fact is grasped. Any attempt to define the "content" of change must include the consequences of pace itself as part of that content.[14]

In a later section of his book, Toffler describes what experimental psychologists call an "orientation response (OR)," "a complex, even massive bodily operation" which occurs when something in our environment is altered.

A few quotes from that portion of *Future Shock* illustrate the theory:

> The level of novelty in our environment has direct physical consequences.
>
> If you overload an environment with novelty, you get the equivalent of anxiety neurotics – people who have their systems continually flooded with adrenaline, continual heart pumping, cold hands, increased muscle tone and tremors – all the usual OR characteristics.
>
> OR happens when we come across novel ideas or information as well as novel sights or sounds. A fresh bit of office gossip, a unifying concept, even a new joke or an original turn of phrase can trigger it.
>
> The OR is particularly stressing when a novel event or fact challenges one's whole preconceived world view.
>
> Novelty, therefore – any perceptible novelty – touches off explosive activity within the body, and especially the nervous system.[15]

It was, then, not so much the changes which upset many Catholics, but the rate of those innovations which disturbed them. We have learned as leaders.

Our diocese over the past several years has introduced a few additional changes: optional communion in the hand, communion under both kinds on Sundays, and guidelines for eucharistic hospitality (occasions when an Episcopal or Protestant Christian is welcome to receive communion in a Catholic church). In these circumstances, however, we took ample time, prepared the clergy first, allowed months for them to absorb the ideas, then, with their help, conducted a diocesan-level instruction program for the general public.

The anxiety level at the end, judging by expressed negative reactions, seems very low. Even those who disagree or prefer not to use the options offered appear satisfied that these innovations have a sound basis or, even lacking that, certainly will not destroy the church they love so dearly.

We made much progress in the seventies, but slipped into a few pitfalls as well, mistakes partially precipitated by the pressures from some to make the revisions as quickly as possible. The insights gleaned from those positive and negative experiences, as well as the orientation they have given us for the eighties, will be the subject of the chapter which follows.

Chapter Three:

A Proper Balance

A capacity community of some 1200 persons gathered in our Cathedral for the funeral liturgy in 1979 of Bishop David F. Cunningham, former ordinary of the Syracuse diocese. The present shepherd, Bishop Frank J. Harrison, delivered the homily and, as normal, during his words there was an absolute stillness throughout the church.

Then the sound of a woman's high heels on the side aisle's tile floor echoed around the old structure. The lady click-clacked her way to the front immediately before the pulpit and bishop, dropped a coin into the votive candle stand, lit a taper, knelt for a private prayer, stood, bowed in the direction of the preacher, made a half-genuflection, and walked back down the same aisle to the rear entrance and out of the building.

As a former associate at this center-city church, I was not surprised by the phenomenon.

We often experienced a similar solo journey during quiet parts of funerals or weddings. Such people had and have a very private, individualized "I" centered notion of prayer, worship and their relationship to God. The woman at Bishop Cunningham's Mass of Christian Burial seemed oblivious to the community assembled for joint prayer and was preoccupied with her needs, her petitions, her candle.

That spirit pervaded much of our pre-Vatican Council liturgy and prayer. The church in its official documents since that point has repeatedly reminded us that, while the individual or the "I" obviously must always be present and provided with space at every public celebration, liturgical worship is essentially a community experience joining diverse people for common prayer, song and gesture.

In the movement to instill more active participation and foster an atmosphere of community, we might ask if our liturgies have not occasionally slipped into the opposite extreme of the pre-Vatican II "I" centered worship.

For example, we can cite the practices in which lectors fail to pause for reflection after readings, celebrants fail to give the community time for personal prayer after the "let us pray," and musicians provide nonstop music at communion. The silent Masses of the past, celebrated according to rubrics that made no provision for silence, have ironically given way to the noisy liturgies of the present whose guidelines call for moments of silence. A public "we" centered notion of prayer, worship and relationship to God, now dominates.

Central to this is the fact that we need to strike a proper balance between these extremes, blending the "I" and the "we" of our worship. We need to integrate the vertical and horizontal dimensions of the liturgy, seeking in this decade to mix the best elements of our pre- and post-Vatican II rituals.

I like to term it a "cross-stamped" approach. We should strive to incorporate into our worship, notions represented by vertical and horizontal bars; the vertical signifying awe, transcendence and private prayer; the horizontal signifying the communal notion of worship. If they succeed in intersecting at the right spot, "cross-stamped," participants will sense there is a deep spirit of prayer to the Father and an atmosphere of genuine concern for one another and others.

At a religious education meeting I attended, an older man talked about something that relates to this correct proportion in the liturgy. He said that we used to fold our hands at Mass but now we hold or shake the hands of our neighbor during the sign of peace, and sometimes during the Our Father. He approves of the new emphasis and enjoys the shaking of hands. But he also questions if we sometimes now fail to fold our hands in worship. In the "cross-stamped" approach, those at worship need to do both.

Finding a middle way, a balanced position between two extremes, is no novelty in the church. Throughout ecclesiastical history, there has been a constant effort to steer a center course both in doctrinal teaching and in pastoral practice. Moreover, whenever one wandered too far in either direction the evil results of false doctrine or poor procedure would eventually surface.

Consider two illustrations of these principles.

Jesus is both son of God and son of Mary, human and divine. Theologians, especially in the early centuries, wrestled with that mystery of Christ and some slipped into exaggerated, erroneous explanations denying either the Lord's divinity or his humanity. The proper doctrine is found in the middle.

The Eucharist is both a sacrifice and a sacrament, reverent worship of the Father and a joyful, sacred meal shared among believing sisters and brothers here on earth. To eliminate or overemphasize either aspect leads to a certain distortion of the liturgy. It becomes either excessively "I" or "we" oriented.

I would now like to explore briefly each of those dimensions.

The vertical dimension of worship.

Ministry, the international journal of the Seventh-day Adventist Ministerial Association, is subtitled "A Magazine for Clergy." In a policy described as "An outstretched hand" the bimonthly is sent to all licensed and/or ordained clergy, even if they have not paid for a subscription or requested it.

The November 1980 issue carried a photo showing the interior of a spacious, Gothic-style church with the caption for a feature article, "Awe – an Essential of Worship."

That story began in this fashion:

> A friend told me that in a certain church he visited, the person offering the morning prayer began by saying, "Good morning, Dad."

> This casual approach to God shocked me, because I have always felt that if a person understands the biblical picture of God and the Creator-creature relationship, he will approach God with a feeling of awe. Awe, it seems to me, is an essential element of worship.

Later in the essay, the author cited instances from the Hebrew scriptures of Nehemiah, Moses and Daniel who "approached God with a sense of reverence that is rare today. They approached him with awe."

He then comments:

> Clearly, awe is a very high emotion. It is one of the emotions that distinguishes humanity from the animal creation. No animal ever looks off into the sunset with wonder and awe in its eyes. Only people do that. I have seen people filled with awe in the presence of a great piece of art, speechless at the skill and the beauty involved in it. I have seen people stand in silence at the edge of the Grand Canyon, awed by the beauty, the enormity, and the impressiveness of the panorama. I have seen people gasping with awe and wonder as they have viewed nature's autumn spectacular of brilliantly colored trees in the New England States. It seems to me that when human beings no longer have a sense of awe in the presence of

God, when awe no longer fills their souls as they worship him, they have lost both the biblical picture of God and an essential element of the worship experience.[1]

Pope John Paul II could only applaud those remarks. On Holy Thursday in 1980 the Holy Father addressed all bishops of the church in a papal letter on the "Mystery and Worship of the Holy Eucharist." In the second section he spoke about the "Sacred Character of the Eucharist and Sacrifice," a sacredness which demands the kind of awesome attitude mentioned by the Seventh-day Adventist writer.

The excerpt below from that portion explains his teaching:

There is a close link between this element of the eucharist and its sacredness, that is to say, its being a holy and sacred action. Holy and sacred, because in it are the continual presence and action of Christ, "the holy one" of God, "anointed with the Holy Spirit," "consecrated by the Father" to lay down his life of his own accord and to take it up again, and the high priest of the new covenant. For it is he who, represented by the celebrant, makes his entrance into the sanctuary and proclaims his Gospel. It is he who is "the offerer and the offered, the consecrator and the consecrated." The eucharist is a holy and sacred action, because it constitutes the sacred species, the Sancta sanctis, that is to say, the "holy things (Christ, the holy one) given to the holy," as all the Eastern liturgies sing at the moment when the eucharistic bread is raised in order to invite the faithful to the Lord's Supper.

The sacred character of the Mass is a sacredness instituted by Christ. The words and action of every priest, answered by the conscious active participation of the whole eucharistic assembly, echo the words and action of Holy Thursday.[2]

From a practical point of view, the appropriate use of silence at liturgies can perhaps as much as any other factor in worship facilitate an atmosphere of awe, sacredness, transcendence and prayer.

There was excessive, although officially unauthorized, silence in pre-Vatican II Masses; one might question if today we are providing inadequate reflective periods at our public worship.

If such is the case, we cannot blame the official guidelines or rubrics. The General Instruction of the Roman Missal clearly expects every liturgy to include moments for silent prayer:

Silence should be observed at designated times as part of the celebration. Its character will depend on the time it occurs in the particular celebration. At the penitential rite and again after the invitation to pray, each one should become recollected; at the conclusion of a reading or homily, each one meditates briefly on what he has heard; after communion, he praises God in his heart and prays.[3]

A congregation will normally not find these silent intervals terribly comfortable when they are first introduced. Our fast-paced, fast-food culture makes us instinctively feel a compulsion to rush ahead and get on with the Mass.

When the priest does pause significantly at "Let us pray," when the lector, cantor or choir waits for the space of an Our Father before moving to the responsorial psalm, when the celebrant sits down while ushers gather the collection and servers prepare the altar, or when the entire community remains seated for reflection after communion, some may muse: "Did he lose his place?" "Why is he waiting?" "Let's get going."

With a little instruction, care and good example from liturgical ministers, especially the priest, who should actually join the people in these pauses, the community will begin to slow down, relax, pray better and understand more clearly this disciplined reflection within the liturgy.

The reason behind our need for awe and reverence at worship, of course, is the fact that we stand before the great mystery of the Eucharist and in the face of other tremendous mysteries of our faith.

Psalm 99 captures some of that majesty with these phrases: "The Lord is king; the peoples tremble. He is throned on the Cherubim; the earth quakes. He is supreme over all the peoples. Let them praise his name, so terrible and great. He is holy, full of power."[4]

Mircea Eliade in his *The Sacred and the Profane* frequently employs the term *mysterium tremendum* about God, a mystery which is tremendous, awe-inspiring, causing us to tremble, arousing a sense of dread within us.[5]

As Roman Catholics we bow down in reverence before many such tremendous mysteries—God, the Trinity, Jesus, the church, the sacraments, the Word and especially the Eucharist. By their very nature as mysteries they are incomprehensible. They never can be fully explained, nor totally grasped, nor perfectly communicated to others.

Conversely, our inner selves are so rich, deep, complex and personal that we cannot adequately put into words for God our interior sentiments of faith, praise, gratitude, petition and repentance.

That double difficulty—the mysteries we reverence and our mysterious spiritual selves seeking to be expressed—has led God, as it were, and humankind into the world of symbols.

Symbols are special kinds of signs. Signs lead us to something beyond, some reality we cannot at this point see or hear or touch. The blinking red railroad sign warns of an approaching train and the lighted exit marker indicates a door to the outside. Symbols do that, and thus we label them as signs, but they possess additional meaning and power which make them mysteries in themselves.

In his classic text, *Models of the Church*, Jesuit Father Avery Dulles treats images and symbols briefly, describing the type of evocative power they possess in a religious context. The theologian's thinking can be seen in this clear and insightful exposition.

> The psychology of images is exceedingly subtle and complex. In the religious sphere, images function as symbols. That is to say, they speak to man existentially and find an echo in the inar-

ticulate depths of his psyche. Such images communicate through their evocative power. They convey a latent meaning that is apprehended in a nonconceptual, even a subliminal, way. Symbols transform the horizons of man's life, integrate his perception of reality, alter his scale of values, reorient his loyalties, attachments, and aspirations in a manner far exceeding the powers of abstract conceptual thought. Religious images, as used in the Bible and Christian preaching, focus our experience in a new way. They have an aesthetic appeal, and are apprehended not simply by the mind but by the imagination, the heart, or, more properly, the whole man.

Any large and continuing society that depends on the loyalty and commitment of its members requires symbolism to hold it together. In secular life, we are familiar with the bald eagle, the black panther, the fleur-de-lis. These images respectively arouse courage, militancy, and purity. The biblical images of the church as the flock of Christ, the bride, the temple, or whatever, operate in a similar manner. They suggest attitudes and courses of action; they intensify confidence and devotion. To some extent they are self-fulfilling; they make the church become what they suggest the church is.[6]

We can draw a few comparisons here to point out the differences between signs and symbols.

• All symbols are signs, but not all signs are symbols.

• Signs supply information, symbols provide inspiration.

• Signs speak to the head, symbols, to the heart.

• Signs are manufactured or discarded, while symbols seem mysteriously to evolve or be created and, in an equally inexplicable way, to lose force or die.

• Signs do not possess hidden power; symbols on the contrary unconsciously work within us evoking strong emotional or spiritual responses.

• Signs have no historical or prophetic content; symbols communicate something of the past, present and future.

The wedding ring is a fine illustration of these concepts. As a sign it simply states: "I am married"; as a symbol, it contains a much deeper, more powerful significance and says: "Someone has, does and will always love me." As a sign, it does not stimulate nor evoke power within us; as a symbol, it can produce tears of grateful remembrance, inspire courage in current temptations and offer hope for an uncertain future.

Marital love and the sacrament of matrimony are realities with all the characteristics of mysteries. The symbolic ring helps humans grasp some of that profound reality, enables us to have a fleeting glimpse of its beauty, makes it possible now and then to touch for a moment this mystery of love which reflects the mystery of God who is love.

In 1978 the United States Bishops' Committee on the Liturgy worked with and approved a document from the Federation of Diocesan Liturgical Commissions entitled *Environment and Art in Catholic Worship.* Opening sentences from its introduction reinforce the ideas we have been suggesting and carry them further along.

> Faith involves a good tension between human modes of expressive communications and God himself, whom our human tools can never adequately grasp. God transcends. God is mystery. God cannot be contained in or confined by any of our words or images or categories.

> While our words and art forms cannot contain or confine God, they can, like the world itself, be icons, avenues of approach, numinous presences, ways of touching without totally grasping or seizing. Flood, fire, the rock, the sea, the mountain, the cloud, the political situations and institutions of succeeding periods—in all of them Israel touched the face of God, found help for discerning a way, moved toward the reign of justice and peace.[7]

This statement notes that the use of symbols in Catholic worship has suffered over the years. Symbols have "tended in practice to shrivel up and petrify," to become "much more manageable and efficient. They still 'caused,' were still 'efficacious,' even though they had often ceased to signify in the richest, fullest sense."[8]

The Liturgy Committee and the Federation judge that in our country proper development of worship and liturgical renewal "requires the opening up of our symbols, especially the fundamental ones of bread and wine, water, oil, the laying on of hands, until we can experience all of them as authentic and appreciate their symbolic value."[9]

There are countless pragmatic applications of those theoretical and general principles to pastoral life. Consider these few examples.

Do lectors proclaim from a large, handsome, decorated book or a missalette or a piece of paper?

Does the celebrant wash his fingers only over a tiny glass receptacle and dry them with an equally tiny linen cloth or does he wash his hands over a basin and dry them with a substantial towel?

Is communion under both kinds offered on a regular pattern at parish Masses?

Are people given, and comfortable with, the laying on of hands in the rites of reconciliation and the anointing of the sick?

Do churches or dioceses accentuate the annual Chrism Mass with its blessing of the oils?

So much of this depends upon the priest or celebrant. The universal church understands that and also knows the training of future clerics holds the key to this growth. In 1979, the Sacred Congregation for Catholic Education issued a lengthy *Instruction on Liturgical Formation in Seminaries.* One of its directives reads:

> It is extremely necessary that the students be taught the art of speaking and of using symbols, as well as how to use communications media. Indeed, in liturgical celebrations it is of the highest importance that the faithful be able to understand the priest, not only in what he says,

whether in the homily or in the prayers and orations, but also in what he does by way of gestures and actions. Formation for this purpose is of such high importance in the renewed liturgy that it deserves very special consideration.[10]

An appendix detailed some items which seemed important to treat in a seminary's liturgical instruction. One spoke specifically of symbols and in words very similar to those of the United States' worship leaders.

> Since the liturgy does not only use words but also signs "chosen by Christ or by the church to signify invisible divine reality," one should speak, in the lessons given, both about gestures and physical bearing as well as about the material things used in liturgical worship. When teaching about the gestures and bearing and their meaning and their power to move souls, one should draw instruction from Sacred Scripture and from the works of the church Fathers. With care, efforts must be made not to allow this teaching to remain abstract, but insure that it filters down to liturgical practice. Even if done briefly, it is helpful to explain singly the meaning, especially the biblical meaning, of the various natural elements used in the liturgy, such as light, water, bread, wine, oil, incense, etc., in particular, those elements which serve as the material of the sacramental signs.[11]

A proper use of disciplined silence and an opening up of symbols are, then, two critical ways for insuring our liturgies possess that vertical dimension of transcendence and prayer.

The horizontal dimension of worship.

An interesting exercise for church leaders is to create an atmosphere of prayer and reflection among a group of parishioners, then read to them the biblical description of early Christian life as found in Acts (2:42-47; 4:32-35). Next ask each person to compare his or her parish with that model, and share the responses with one another.

> They devoted themselves to the apostles' instruction and the communal life, to the breaking of bread and the prayers.
>
> A reverent fear overtook them all, for many wonders and signs were performed by the apostles. Those who believed shared all things in common; they would sell their property and goods, dividing everything on the basis of each one's need. They went to the temple area together every day, while in their homes they broke bread. With exultant and sincere hearts they took their meals in common, praising God and winning the approval of all the people. Day by day the Lord added to their number those who were being saved.[12]

The thread of community life – common prayer, meals, even property – certainly shines through this account of those first Christian clusters. The members recognized each other as brothers and sisters in the Lord, incorporated the horizontal dimension into public worship, and understood the "we" aspect of liturgy.

The council fathers accepted that concept as one of the norms to govern the reform of our worship. In their words, "Liturgical services are not private functions but are celebrations of the church which is 'the sacrament of unity,' namely, 'the holy people united and arranged under their bishops.' Therefore, liturgical services pertain to the whole Body of Christ."[13]

Pope John Paul II, in that Holy Thursday letter which stressed the sacred character of the Mass, also noted the strong community aspect of the Eucharist.

> But the church is not brought into being only through the union of people, through the experience of brotherhood to which the eucharistic banquet gives rise. The church is brought into being when, in that fraternal union and communion, we celebrate the sacrifice of the cross of Christ, when we proclaim "the Lord's death until he comes," and later, when, being deeply compenetrated with the mystery of our salvation, we approach as a community the table of the Lord, in order to be nourished there, in a sacramental manner, by the fruits of the holy sacrifice of propitiation. Therefore in eucharistic communion we receive Christ, Christ himself; and our union with him, which is a gift and grace for each individual, brings it about that in him we are also associated in the unity of his body which is the church.[14]

A frequently used aphorism is pertinent here: The church makes the Eucharist; the Eucharist makes the church.

What we believe affects the way we worship. How we pray liturgically reflects the beliefs behind our prayer life. Our understanding of church, therefore, will influence the expression of church in our liturgies. A shift in our perception of what church means will consequently and necessarily bring out a modification in the way we worship.

During the first part of this century Catholics generally held a heavily institutional view of the church. As a result, the approach to liturgy was often in exclusively external, rubrical terms, despite the growing liturgical movement which sought to revive and reform both our outlook and our rituals.

During World War II, however, Pope Pius XII, in the publication of his encyclical on the Mystical Body of Christ, provided both a new theological orientation toward the church and, at the same time, official, theoretical support for this community concept of the liturgy.

The church, thus, was not only or merely buildings, rules and organizational structures, but more – sisters and brothers linked together by grace to form a living organism, the Body of Christ. This real, living inner unity would naturally flow over into the way we prayed and worshiped.

St. Paul's words about the Body of Christ, of course, served as the biblical basis for this concept and Jesus' comments about the vine and branches expressed the same teaching with a different figure.

The Second Vatican Council built upon these ideas and developed our understanding of the church as the holy, convenanted People of God. Starting with the prophet Jeremiah (31: 31-34), the Fathers saw the notion's culmination in this famous text from the first epistle of Peter:

> You, however, are "a chosen race, a royal priesthood, a holy nation, a people he claims for his own to proclaim the glorious works" of the One who called you from darkness into his marvelous light. Once you were no people, but now you are God's people . . . (1 Peter 2: 9-10).

Just as our awareness of God's transcendence leads to a vertical dimension of liturgy, so, too, our appreciation of the church as Christ's body and God's people brings us to the horizontal or communal aspect of worship.

From a practical standpoint, maximum involvement by members of the worshiping unit in the planning, preparing and executing of liturgies is an absolutely crucial step for the proper growth of that community element.

The church lends authoritative backing to this measure both in its general liturgical directives and in very specific regulations for each ritual. The pragmatic wisdom of this insistence becomes evident in a comparison with an experience outside the church scene. If I purchase or inherit a few shares of stock in some company, I suddenly become interested in the firm's progress. I check the market each day and follow closely the business's quarterly reports. I have part ownership now and am more vitally concerned with the company's life and future.

In a parallel fashion, those who get involved in a worship service experience a deeper meaning. Their interest is more fully engaged when couples plan their nuptial ceremony, when parents proclaim the scriptures at their infant's baptism, when children construct a banner for a special Mass, when volunteers assist the ill at a communal anointing celebration, or when confirmation candidates wear garments they have made.

We have witnessed an enormous growth during the past decade in this type of active liturgical involvement. It needs to be maintained as well as expanded both in quantity and quality.

There are some weak areas which require special care in the years ahead. Preparation of funeral liturgies is one of them.

The Introduction to the *Rite of Funerals* explicitly directs the celebrant to involve the family in planning the Mass of Christian Burial and other burial rituals. For example, it states:

> The priest should consider the various circumstances and in particular the wishes of the family and the community (Article 23).

> In general, all the texts are interchangeable and may be chosen, with the help of the community or family, to reflect the individual sitution (Article 24:1).

> The priest should . . . show loving concern for the family of the deceased person, support them in the time of sorrow, and as much as possible involve them in planning the funeral celebration and the choice of options made available in the rite (Article 25:3).

There are suitable pastoral aids available to fulfill those directives, but my observations indicate that this kind of desirable planning takes place only in a minority of situations. It demands added time and effort from the celebrant, requirements which can be eased by the development of a competent parish "bereaved-ministry committee" that may assist the priest in this noble work. The spiritual rewards from such added effort for all concerned will be immediately evident.

A second measure critical for fostering the horizontal dimension of worship is the concerted, varied attempt to create a warm, inviting climate of hospitality at the liturgy.

In recent years Catholic churches in the United States seem to have lost members, many from the larger, often impersonal parishes, to smaller, more intimate evangelical congregations. They need to belong, to be known, to be cared for or about, but found these qualities missing in Catholic churches. One detects increasing efforts today to build up that kind of hospitable atmosphere in our parishes.

Celebrants meeting people at the doors, greeters welcoming all and identifying strangers, parish councils and pastors constructing weekday chapels designed to save energy and draw the few worshipers together physically, are a few examples.

Maximum involvement by members of the community in the liturgy, and combined attempts to build a climate of hospitality are, then, two important ways of fostering that horizontal or communal aspect of worship.

However, we should mention that reluctance to abandon old ways upon the part of many Catholics has made the move from the individualistic, private approach to a communitarian, public stance in worship neither easy nor totally successful. In my judgment, that resistance will continue to serve as a major obstacle in the way of full, fruitful participation for years to come.

The one necessary ingredient, nevertheless, remains a sense of balance, the proper perspective – the delicate combination of both the vertical and horizontal, the "I" and the "we."

Near the end of the document, *Norms on Eucharistic Practices,* the Congregation for the Sacraments and Divine Worship maintains the same point and with identical words. Its summary of that position is quoted from one of the finest passages of the *Constitution on the Sacred Liturgy,* and forms a fitting conclusion to this discussion:

> The liturgy also requires great balance, for as the constitution *Sacrosanctum Concilium* says, it "is thus the outstanding means by which the faithful can express in their lives, and manifest to others, the mystery of Christ and the real nature of the true church. It is of the essence of the church that she be both human and divine, visible and yet invisibly endowed, eager to act and yet devoted to contemplation, present in this world and yet not at home in it. She is all these things in such a way that in her the human is directed and subordinated to the divine, the visible likewise to the

invisible, action to contemplation and this present world to that city yet to come, which we seek." Without this balance, the true face of Christian liturgy becomes obscured.[15]

Part II:

The Mass:
A Review for
Liturgical Ministers
and Leaders

Introduction

This book has grown out of several conferences given to priests in my home diocese of Syracuse.

When the Roman document *Norms on Eucharistic Practices* appeared, it seemed a wise idea to offer our clergy an update and review of the rubrics for Mass. They had been celebrating liturgies according to the revised order of Mass for a decade and we judged a swift glance at some salient developments might prove helpful at this time.

In preparation I went rather carefully through the *Norms on Eucharistic Practices,* the General Instruction of the Roman Missal, a Foreword and an Appendix to that text issued by the National Conference of Catholic Bishops, as well as several other official decrees. In addition, I tried to pull together my own observations of liturgies over recent years and those pastoral suggestions which enjoy near universal support.

The goal was to present for priests, deacons, liturgical ministers and worship planners a kind of check list highlighting points which possess clear official approbation and sound practical value.

Such a "rubrical" lecture by its nature deals mainly with externals, the "how to" dimension of liturgy. One would not expect the dry, generally legalistic presentation to capture an audience's vivid attention. I was, therefore, very surprised at each of the four locations to have the crowd, almost totally priests, listen carefully and pose a good many questions.

The explanation of that attentiveness probably rests in the fact that this check list approach formed an examination of conscience for the celebrants. Each man apparently made the talk personal, reflecting on how he offers Mass—if he does this or has slipped into that—and what suggestions might be applicable to his own parish setting.

Following one session, our regional episcopal vicar for that sector expressed a desire to have these comments in writing. The positive responses and his request gave me inspiration and encouragement to write this book.

The chapters which follow will look at the four parts of the Mass and give a check list of items which appear in need of treatment. They do not cover every word or gesture of a eucharistic liturgy and thus will not teach a new liturgical minister the precise details of how to celebrate worship. At the same time, while these are more of a review, any person involved in planning, leadership or ministry roles could find them valuable for development of creative liturgies.

As far as possible, we have listed in footnotes the official documentation for the points covered.

Chapter Four:

Introductory Rites

The part preceding the liturgy of the word, namely, the entrance song, greeting, penitential rite, Kyrie, Gloria and opening prayer or collect, have the character of beginning, introduction and preparation.

The purpose of these rites is to make the assembled people a unified community and to prepare them properly to listen to God's word and celebrate the eucharist.[1]

The Roman Missal, General Instruction

• Only one cross in the sanctuary, on, near or above the altar, is the most desirable. A processional cross with a floor standard has many advantages over one permanently hung or fixed to a wall. When the processional cross is not used at the altar, it should be put away. While permissible to have the cross on the altar, the United

States Bishops' Committee on the Liturgy in its document *Environment and Art in Catholic Worship* suggests it would be preferable elsewhere so that the altar is used only for bread and wine and book. There would be no need, for example, to have a small cross on the altar in a church with a large crucifix attached to the wall or hanging from the ceiling.[2]

• The candles may, but need not be on the altar. In fact, greater visibility and freedom would give preference for their placement off the altar. For exposition of the Blessed Sacrament, it should be noted that only two, four or six candles are lighted, as at Mass. The older candelabra with a dozen or so tapers silently make a value judgment about the priority of exposition over the eucharistic celebration. The church has corrected that in its *Holy Communion and Worship of the Eucharist Outside Mass.*[3]

• The altar should be clear of everything before the celebration begins. That simplified state emphasizes the basic richness of the altar symbolism and eliminates the visual distraction of objects on the altar. We have evident failings in this regard. It is very common to see a multitude of books, missalettes, papers, cruets and other items cluttering the Lord's table prior to Mass.

The altar is the table of the Lord and the people of God are called to share in this table. It likewise symbolizes Christ and accordingly should be the most noble, the most beautifully designed and constructed table the community can provide. At the beginning of the liturgy of the Eucharist the Lord's table is prepared as the center of the action to follow. Servers unfold the corporal upon it and likewise place there the vessels needed. To do so beforehand and have those items on the altar from the beginning destroys entirely the rich symbolism intended by the church.

• "Any book which is used by an officiating minister in a liturgical celebration should be of a large (public, noble) size, good paper, strong design, handsome typography and binding. The Book of the Gospels or lectionary, of course, is central and should be handled and carried in a special way. The other liturgical books of the church, which contain the rites of our public worship tradition, are also worthy of venerable treatment and are a significant part of the liturgical environment. Each should be visually attractive and impressive. The use of pamphlets and leaflets detracts from the visual integrity of the total liturgical action."[4]

This is a recommendation frequently ignored in parishes. Priests use missalettes for prayers at the presidential chair, lectors do the same for readings at the lectern and celebrants employ pamphlets or paperbacks during sacramental rituals.

At the Miami "Faith and Fiesta" music and worship conference in 1980, the planners discovered or developed a large lectionary handsomely decorated with an ikon of the Lord, the kind of noble book urged above.

- "When a liturgical book is employed at a place other than altar or ambo, the book should be held by an assistant or acolyte so that the hands and body of the one who reads are free."[5]

This and other guidelines really challenge those who maintain altar servers no longer have value. Among the important functions of a server in good worship are caring for the needed articles, holding the sacramentary for prayers, preparing the altar and clearing it, and processing with cross and candles. Thus the server continues to have a significant role in our revised liturgies.

- Priests, parish ministers and members of a hospitality committee who greet worshipers arriving at the door help lift people out of their isolation and usher them into the community spirit necessary for good liturgy. This ministry of welcome may be even more important than greeting the people after Mass.

A permanent or temporary vestry space near the main entrance greatly facilitates that task, particularly for the priest celebrant.

- The chalice placed on a table other than the altar beforehand "should be covered with a veil, which may always be white."[6]

- Our eyes should naturally focus on the main sanctuary elements of altar, chair and lectern. A sanctuary filled with a variety of unneeded chairs, kneelers, tables and candles distracts us from that proper view or perspective. In the words of the American bishops: This "in-

vites a thorough house cleaning in which super-
fluities, things that have no use or are no longer
used, are removed. Both beauty and simplicity
demand careful attention to each piece of fur-
niture, each object, each decorative element, as
well as to the whole assembly, so that there is no
clutter, no crowding. These various objects and
elements must be able to breathe and function
without being smothered by excess."[7]

As an experiment, the parish liturgy committee with the priest(s) might look at the sanctuary,
even take a photograph of the scene. Then they
should remove all the items not truly needed, that
is, extra kneelers, candles, chairs, missalettes.
Also place at a distance or out of view, elements
of lesser significance, for example, credence table,
ablution cup. Finally, the group should examine
the simplified setting and photograph it. The
truth of this section will probably become self-
evident.

• A brief prayer before the entrance procession begins can help the liturgical ministers focus
on the worship service and lead them into a proper attitude of awe before the transcendent
mysteries they are about to celebrate.

This can take several forms: a silent reflective
pause, a simple invitation from the celebrant to
reflect on the coming liturgy, or spontaneous
petitions from those who wish to make them.[8]

• The purpose of the entrance procession and
song "is to open the celebration, deepen the unity
of the people, introduce them to the mystery of

the season or feast, and accompany the procession."[9] While the procession can be worked out in a number of ways, the song should be continued beyond one verse and sustained long enough for the congregation to really get into it. No doubt we need a balance between the Catholic "one verse only" approach, and the Protestant practice of "singing all the verses printed, no matter how long." Regardless of that difficulty, a hymn, psalm or other alternative, sung at the entrance, should be the usual practice.

• When there is no song at the entrance, it has become the regular procedure for the congregation to recite the brief antiphon from the missal as it appears in popular participation booklets. This is a legitimate option because it can be recited "either by the people, by some of them, or by a reader."

Another permissible option is found in the General Instruction of the Roman Missal where it says, "Otherwise it (the brief antiphon) is said by the priest after the greeting."[10] The American bishops in their foreword to the Roman Missal indicate both that variation and the reason behind it.

"Since these antiphons are too abrupt for communal recitation, it is preferable when there is no singing that the priest (or the deacon, other minister, or commentator) adopt the antiphon and incorporate it in the presentation of the Mass of the day. After the initial greeting, 'the priest, deacon, or other minister may very briefly introduce the Mass of the day' (*Order of Mass,* no. 3). The adaptation of the text of the entrance antiphon for this purpose is suggested by the Congregation for Divine Worship."[11]

The procedure by which a lector says, "Please join with me in reciting the entrance antiphon on page __ of your missalette" has become so common that most priests and people, in my opinion, consider it required by liturgical law. As the bishops have indicated, however, these sentences are so short that they make little sense by themselves and when recited by the entire congregation.

Their alternate recommendation is for the celebrant (or someone else) after his greeting to introduce briefly the Mass, including the antiphon or an adapted form of it within his introduction. For example, on the feast of the Holy Family, the priest (or another) might say:

"We celebrate today the feast of the Holy Family. These words from St. Luke's gospel set the scene for our liturgy: 'The shepherds hastened to Bethlehem, where they found Mary and Joseph, and the baby lying in a manger.' Let us look into our hearts, repent of all sin, and ask the Lord who came to save us to forgive our failures as we prepare for this celebration."

• After venerating the altar and moving to the presidential chair, the priest might consider a simple "good morning" or "good afternoon" to the congregation. Moreover, in a large parish, or on a major feast with many visitors present, or at a special communal anointing or penance celebration in which there is a unique configuration of people, he could invite participants to turn and greet their neighbors. I can speak from ten years' experience about the positive value of this very simple, workable and effective procedure. It relaxes the congregation and develops, even if in a minimal way, a greater sense of belonging and community.

Some may argue that this duplicates the formal, apostolic greeting provided in the rubrics. I disagree. People generally arrive for Mass in an isolated, individualistic, preoccupied frame of mind. The very human greeting and introductions outlined above help break through those shells or walls and make persons more conscious of each other. They will then receive with deeper attention and meaning the official, biblical greeting addressed to them precisely as a unique Christian gathering or assembly.

• Veneration of the altar and the sign of the cross are extremely significant gestures which should be carried out slowly with great care and reverence.

• The penitential rite includes several options. Form C basically consists of acclamations which praise the Lord and implore his mercy.[12] They are a series of invocations addressed to Christ and were traditionally a prayer of praise to the risen Jesus.[13] The Missal contains eight versions for use and as models.

The praiseworthy practice of composing such

acclamations has, however, been marred by the unfortunate development of making these into a litany of faults. "For the times we have . . ." By simply reading through those in the sacramentary, liturgy planners will both see how inappropriate are these recitations of failings and understand how to construct suitable invocations.

• Neither the priest nor the people make the sign of the cross at the absolution which concludes the penitential rite. The council fathers decreed: "The rites should be distinguished by a noble simplicity; they should be short, clear and unencumbered by useless repetitions. . . ."[14] That meant eliminating almost all of the 50 plus signs of the cross previously required by the rubrics and leaving only three: at the beginning of Mass, over the gifts and at the dismissal, with an additional one in the first eucharistic prayer.

• The priest's invitation to the community to pray can take several forms: a simple: "Let us pray"; the addition from the Missal of the expanded version in parentheses ("that we will be guided by the light of faith"); a planned or spontaneous personalized formula ("Let us pray on this feast of Epiphany that we may experience the joy which comes from discovering Christ in our lives").

Here and in other similar greetings, the celebrant may use a variety of salutations, for example, "Friends," "My dear people," "Brothers and sisters." As a sign of lingual sensitivity to the presence of women in the community, the use of "brothers *and* sisters" clearly is desirable. Inverting the order to "sisters and brothers" manifests an added awareness. I like to interchange these throughout the liturgy, at one point using "brothers and sisters" and, at another, "sisters and brothers."

• "The priest invites the people to pray, and together they spend some moments in silence so they may realize that they are in God's presence and may make their petitions."[15]

The American bishops have added this commentary: "The period of silence will be richer, and demand sufficient time, so that the people can actually pray. Silence then becomes a real and meaningful part of the celebration. The brief, optional expansion of the invitatory structures the silence and helps people to be aware of the petitionary character of the opening prayer. If the priest uses his own words, the invitatory can be more concrete and effective."[16]

Pausing for an insufficient amount of time after the invitation and before proclaiming the opening prayer may well be the most frequent fault of current celebrants.

Pope John Paul II modeled the proper approach during the beatification Mass for Blessed Kateri Tekakwitha. He invited all at St. Peter's to pray, joined hands and paused for a lengthy period of silent prayer, then sang the oration.

• As noted above, a server should hold the

book so the priest may be free to extend his hands and join them during the opening prayer experience.

• When the prayer is completed, the server should carry the sacramentary away in a dignified manner and place it off by the side on the credence table until needed later on at the altar.

Now gathered together as a Christian community, everyone, including the priest, is seated, prepared to hear with faith and love God's inspired word.

Chapter Five:

Liturgy of the Word

Readings from scripture and the chants between the readings form the main part of the liturgy of the word. The homily, profession of faith, and general intercessions or prayer of the faithful develop and complete it. In the readings, explained by the homily, God speaks to his people of redemption and salvation and nourishes their spirit; Christ is present among the faithful through his word. Through the chants the people make God's word their own and express their adherence to it through the profession of faith. Finally, moved by this word, they pray in the general intercessions for the needs of the Church and for the world's salvation.[1]

The Roman Missal, General Instruction

• When the lectionary was first introduced in 1969, the National Conference of Catholic

Bishops decided that the pattern of three biblical readings on Sundays and feast days would be observed in the United States.

However, for Masses involving special groups, the American bishops provided wide latitude in the selection of scriptural texts. The celebrant and his planning committee may choose "from the readings of that week"; they may also look to "readings not found in the current week, provided they are from the approved lectionary, and appropriate to the particular celebration, and are not chosen to the disadvantage of the ordinary use of the weekday lectionary."[2]

Moreover, the 1973 Roman *Directory for Masses with Children* goes even further: "If three or even two readings on Sundays or weekdays can be understood by children only with difficulty, it is permissible to read two or only one of them, but the reading of the gospel should never be omitted."[3]

Finally, there is no obligation to have three scriptural readings at weddings, funerals or on other similar occasions.

In summary, the church offers great freedom in selecting the appropriate biblical excerpts for Masses outside of Sundays and major feasts. My observations indicate that a major challenge for current parish liturgists is simply taking advantage of the lectionary's already rich resources. The reference table in the back of the volume makes it a relatively easy task to coordinate a passage from one's personal bible with the corresponding excerpt in the lectionary.

• "It would be a serious abuse to replace the word of God with the word of man, no matter who the author may be."[4] This prohibition against substituting non-scriptural readings for biblical texts at Mass merely repeats Vatican directives issued a decade earlier.[5]

While restating the admonition, Pope John Paul II in his 1980 Holy Thursday letter nevertheless suggested how non-scriptural excerpts could "be used very profitably in the homily. Indeed the homily is supremely suitable for the use of such texts provided their content corresponds to the required conditions, since it is one of the tasks that belong to the nature of the homily to show the point of convergence between revealed wisdom and noble human thought seeking the truth by various paths."[6]

A priest or deacon should read the gospel. If another priest is present and no deacon, the other priest rather than the celebrant should proclaim the gospel while the celebrant listens attentively. A formally instituted lector, spiritually and technically trained for the task, should read the other texts.[7] As noted below, it is desirable to have as many readers as readings, thus normally two on Sunday.

Even on weekdays it is highly desirable to involve one of the participants in this function as the proclaimer of the word.

Sulpician Father Eugene Walsh has some very practical suggestions for placement of readers during a celebration:

It is an important sign that readers be seated at Sunday Mass in the church with the rest of the people. There is no reason for readers to be seated in the sanctuary all during the celebration. It is a question of sign again. The presence of readers in their own place is a first sign of the "people" status of their ministry. This sign is further enhanced when they are seen going from their own place to read and returning to their own place when they have finished. Also, they should sit together with their families or other companions rather than in some sort of isolation.

It is important also that there be as many readers as there are readings. The principle of "people" ministries should be: increase and multiply, not diminish. It is becoming very clear to many in the church that development of these new ministries is one of the most important energies in the growth of the church today and tomorrow.

One of the readers carries the book (lectionary or bible) in the opening procession. He or she places the book closed on the lectern and returns to place.

At the time for the first reading, the people are sitting down after the prayer. The reader does not sit, but remains standing in place for a moment until there is quiet. This helps avoid the see-saw effect, the catapulting of reader into the reading space from the seated group.

Let there be a moment's pause. We are beginning the first really important part of the celebration. Up to this point all has been preliminary. The reader moves directly to the lectern. She (he) moves with energy and dignity, not too fast, not too slow, and does not stop to bow or genuflect. The sign of the reader moving to place is itself an excellent sign announcing to the entire celebrating community that it is time to get ready. This sign helps to begin calling the people to attention.[8]

• It is critical that the celebrant look at and listen to the lector during the proclamation of God's word. Reading along in the missalette or, worse, looking over the community and "counting the house" is both rude and a visual distraction. These will tend to focus the congregation's eyes and attention on the priest instead of upon the reader. By concentrating on the proclaimer, the priest offers a model for those in the pews.

• The lectionaries for each of the three Sunday cycles that are published by Pueblo Co., in my experience have proven to be excellent books for diffident lectors. The size, print, accented words, sense lines and clarity of the texts will lead lectors to use them instead of a pamphlet or typed sheet.[9]

• The responsorial psalm, an integral part of the liturgy of the word, may not be omitted even if not sung. Ideally, however, it should be chanted by the cantor or psalmist who is the proper person to render this text, not the lector. In point of fact, many, probably most, American parishes have not reached that point of musical implementation of the responsorial psalm.

The assigned psalm may be replaced by another one, a practice which might serve well a church in the beginning stages of learning how to sing the psalms. The community can quickly learn the simple antiphonal responses to the common responsorial psalms and within a year's time thus have a repertoire of available psalms for use at Sunday Masses.

• The celebrant or deacon's prayer before the gospel should be recited quietly, not in a tone to be heard by the people.

• A period of silent pause for reflection after each reading can be "active, integrating and transforming," yet, as noted, is often omitted in American parishes.[10]

• The alleluia or the verse before the gospel may be omitted, if not sung.[11] Father Eugene Walsh, a well-known liturgist and musician, goes a step further and urges: "Unless it is sung, the Alleluia Acclamation is omitted. Alleluias are for singing."[12]

• The *Newsletter* of the Bishops' Committee on the Liturgy points out that "In addition to the distinct (ordained) minister, the gospel book may be set apart by other signs of reverence. It is carried in procession, placed upon the altar, accompanied by acolytes with candles, and incensed. Out of respect, the assembly stands during the reading of the sacred text and after the proclamation, the book is reverently kissed by the minister."[13]

In Holy Sepulcher Church, Butler, Pennsylvania, a movable candle stands on each side of the lectern throughout the liturgy of the word.

During preparations for the liturgy of the Eucharist, servers move the candles to a spot near the altar.

Father Lucien Deiss highly recommends a gospel procession with appropriate music to highlight the dignity of God's word. He demonstrated that teaching at the major Mass for the Miami's "Faith and Fiesta" conference and included liturgical dance as part of the alleluia acclamation.

• "The purpose of the homily is to explain to the faithful the word of God proclaimed in the readings and to apply its message to the present."[14]

The homilist needs to avoid two extreme positions here.

One totally ignores the scriptural texts of the Mass. I recall while on vacation listening to a quite competent, well-prepared and rather popular preacher. The sermon was good and pertinent, but had absolutely no explicit nor even implicit connection with any of the biblical readings of that liturgy.

The other ignores an application of the readings to the present. This approach either retells the biblical story, paraphrases what has been already read or exegetes the scriptural texts. The retelling and paraphrasing are deadly mistakes; the exegesis is valuable and praiseworthy, but incomplete.

If that popular preacher and the scholarly exegete could pool their talents, the result could be a model homily.

• The *Norms on Eucharistic Practices,* having described the nature of a homily, concludes "that it is to be given by priests and deacons only. Significantly the Latin text uses the technical term *munus* in stating that it is the office or function of the ordained minister to preach. This suggests activity (rather than a dignity) proper to ordination exercised for the sake of others (i.e., the faithful). Thus, it is ordination that gives a person the *munus* (office) to preach, the exercise of which depends further on canonical mission. This paragraph, with its emphasis on proper *munus* linked to ordination, maintains the distinction between clergy and laity as basic in terms of who may preach. No consideration is given, therefore, to those situations where, in terms of proper theological training, there are lay persons who would appear to be qualified to preach to the community within the liturgical celebration.

"Reference should be made to the 1971 response of the Pontifical Commission for the Interpretation of Decrees of the Second Vatican Council. Commenting on the words of the *General Instruction* (no. 42) that 'the homily should ordinarily be given by the celebrant himself' it stated that it could not be so interpreted as to allow laymen and women to preach at the eucharistic liturgy. This response affirms that the ministry (*primum officium*) is exercised in communion with the local bishop. It is not intended to show the hierarchy in opposition to the laity.

"Finally, reference must be made to the 1973 *Directory for Masses with Children* where it is permitted to have an adult other than the priest or deacon explain the gospel to the children when the ordinary minister does not feel qualified to address children."[15] That permission was not contravened by the 1980 instruction.

The General Instruction's directive that the homily ordinarily should be given by the celebrant himself raises questions about a practice fairly common in large churches with several resident priests. In those situations the clergy often work out an alternating schedule in which one preacher speaks at all the Masses on a given weekend.

The Missal would seem to discourage that. However, it also permits one of the concelebrants to preach at a concelebrated Eucharist. Moreover, deacons are authorized to preach, and when a bishop presides another cleric besides the celebrant frequently delivers the homily. Legally, then, the regulation about the celebrant ordinarily being the preacher does not seem to be so restrictive as to exclude this alternating procedure.

As one who has followed both systems for a long period of time – preaching every week at the Masses I celebrated and preaching every second, third or fourth week at all the weekend liturgies – I prefer for practical, pastoral reasons the staggered schedule arrangement. A later chapter in this book will suggest reasons for that preference and ways to maximize the celebrant's participation in someone else's homily.

After the introduction to the gospel, the priest or deacon "makes the sign of the cross with his thumb on the book and on his forehead, mouth and breast."[16] Both priests and people can be reminded to make crosses that clearly are crosses – made visibly, slowly and reverently.

• At the end of the gospel, the one who has proclaimed the text "kisses the book, saying *quietly*: 'May the words of the gospel wipe away our sins.' "[17]

• A sign of the cross should *not* begin or conclude the homily. The homily flows out of the gospel and leads into the profession of faith or general intercessions. A sign of the cross before and after isolates the homily and is a carry-over from earlier days when there was little or no connection between the scriptural texts, the sermon and the liturgy. Furthermore, it violates the norm cited earlier which urged a noble simplicity and the elimination of useless repetitions.

• "The homily is given at the chair or at the lectern," but it would also seem appropriate at other places in the sanctuary if pastoral reasons indicate the word would be preached more effectively at such a location where the homilist can be best seen and heard.[18]

• It is helpful and desirable in preparing liturgies to involve parishioners as homily helpers and general intercession writers.

• During the profession of faith at the words: "by the power of the Holy Spirit, etc.," all bow;

when these phrases occur on the feasts of the Annunciation or Christmas, all genuflect.[19]

"The two parts which in a sense go to make up the Mass, namely the liturgy of the word and the eucharistic liturgy, are so closely connected that they form but one single act of worship. A person should not approach the table of the bread of the Lord without having first been at the table of his word."[20] We have experienced through faith Christ, present in his inspired word; now we move on to encounter the risen Jesus in the liturgy of the Eucharist.

Chapter Six:

Liturgy of the Eucharist

At the Last Supper Christ instituted the paschal sacrifice and meal. In this meal the sacrifice of the cross is continually made present in the Church when the priest, representing Christ, carries out what the Lord did and handed over to his disciples to do in his memory.

Christ took bread and the cup, gave thanks, broke, and gave to his disciples, saying: "Take and eat, this is my body. Take and drink, this is the cup of my blood. Do this in memory of me." The Church has arranged the celebration of the eucharistic liturgy to correspond to these words and actions of Christ:

1) In the preparation of the gifts, bread, wine and water are brought to the altar, the same elements which Christ used.

2) The eucharistic prayer is the hymn of thanksgiving to God for the whole work of salvation; the offerings become the body and blood of Christ.

3) The breaking of the one bread is a sign of the unity of the faithful, and in communion they receive the body and blood of Christ as the Apostles did from his hands.

The Roman Missal, General Instruction[1]

• A sound liturgical principle is that in worship no two actions should be carried on simultaneously. A good illustration of violating that norm often occurs at the beginning of the liturgy of the Eucharist when the celebrant moves to the altar and starts the Preparation of the Gifts while the ushers take up the collection. This practice minimizes the spiritual dimensions of the financial gifts and also weakens the congregation's ability to reflect or concentrate on the altar actions.

Here is a procedure in accord with the rubrics and proven pastorally successful over many years on the parish level:

a) Immediately after the general intercessions all, including the celebrant, are seated.

b) Ushers without delay come forward and distribute the baskets "to collect money or gifts for the poor and the Church."[2] Baskets which must be passed from person to person are preferable to those with handles held by ushers because of the more active involvement required.

c) At the same time, servers prepare the Lord's table as the center of the eucharistic liturgy by placing the corporal, purificator, chalice and missal on it.[3]

d) The organist, choir, folk group or other instrumentalists provide some appropriate musical background during these events.

e) When the collection has been gathered, some participants, ideally selected beforehand and if possible their names indicated in the bulletin, bring forward the offerings together with the bread and wine.

f) The celebrant and servers move to the sanctuary's edge and accept the gifts. The bread and wine are taken to the altar; the donations for the poor and the church are "laid in a suitable place but not on the altar."[4] It is highly desirable for the celebrant to be a contributor himself and drop his own envelope in the basket of offerings.

• If the offertory antiphon is not sung, it is omitted, a procedure almost universally followed in our country.[5]

• The offertory song which may accompany the procession and preparation of the gifts "is not always necessary or desirable. Organ or instrumental music is also fitting at the time. When song is used it is to be noted that the song need not speak of bread and wine or of offering. The proper function of this song is to accompany and celebrate the communal aspects of the procession. The text, therefore, can be any appropriate song of praise or of rejoicing in keeping with the season. . . . Instrumental interludes can effectively accompany the procession . . . and thus keep this part of the Mass in proper perspective relative to the eucharistic prayer which follows."[6]

It is really not very feasible for participants

simultaneously to open up their pocketbooks or wallets, pass the basket, hold the hymnal, turn the pages and sing. For these reasons, choral or instrumental background music seems more suitable. It also gives the community an opportunity to rest, reflect upon the word spoken and prepare to concentrate on the eucharistic prayer which follows.

• A few parishes do not take up the collection, but have receptacles at the main entrances for members to deposit their offering as they arrive for Mass. I prefer the procedure outlined above because of its deeper involvement and spiritual, symbolic dimension.

• Rather than term this the offertory or the offertory procession, the church calls these actions the Preparation of the Altar and Procession with the Gifts. The true offertory occurs after the institutional narrative or consecration when we offer Christ, the sacrifice and victim to our Father in the Spirit.[7]

• Incense, as "a symbol of the church's offering and prayer going up to God," has tended to be used less in liturgies over the past decade, but remains a legitimate option at the usual times and may be due for a rise in popularity.[8]

Good worship involves the whole person, our body as well as our spirit self. Thus we need to express inner qualities of faith and prayerfulness not only in thoughts and words, but likewise in non-verbal symbols (e.g., incense and rising smoke) and ritual gestures (e.g., incensing the cross, gifts, altar, ministers and people) which we can see, hear, touch and smell.

Both the *Directory for Masses with Children* (sections 33-36) and the document on *Environment and Art in Catholic Worship* (sections 12-15, 55-62) treat the matter of non-verbal symbols and ritual gestures at some length and in a practical way.

• If there is singing or music during the Preparation of Gifts, the celebrant recites the "Blessed are you, Lord God . . ." prayers quietly. He should not wait for the conclusion of singing before moving on with this Preparation of Gifts.

• The paten and bread as well as the chalice are only raised "slightly above the altar" or "a little" as the celebrant recites the accompanying prayer.[9]

• The other prayers at the Preparation of Gifts are recited quietly, not in a tone to be heard by the people.[10]

• When there are several chalices or containers of wine on the altar, the water needs to be added to only one, the central vessel.

• The use of the pall is optional.[11]

• After the people's response to "Pray, brethren" (better brothers and sisters, sisters and brothers or friends), the priest does not say "Amen" or pause for silence, but moves immediately to the prayer over the gifts.[12]

• Since the Second Vatican Council, many persons seeking to implement the directives of the new Roman Missal developed more substantial altar breads. These better approximated actual bread and could be broken at the Lamb of God for distribution to at least some of the congregation. The basis for those efforts was this paragraph from the General Instruction:

> The nature of the sign demands that the material for the eucharistic celebration appear as actual food. The eucharistic bread, even though unleavened and traditional in form, should therefore be made in such a way that the priest can break it and distribute the parts to at least some of the faithful. When the number of communicants is large or other pastoral needs require it, small hosts may be used. The gesture of the breaking of the bread, as the eucharist was called in apostolic times, will more clearly show the eucharist as a sign of unity and charity, since the one bread is being distributed among the members of one family.[13]

A wide variety of recipes which were worked out included additives like honey, molasses, salt, sugar and shortening. Those were necessary so that what was considered an unleavened loaf might be in accord with these norms of the *Third Instruction on the Correct Implementation of the Constitution on the Sacred Liturgy:*

> The necessity for the sign to be genuine applies more to the colour, taste and texture of the bread than to its shape. Out of reverence for the sacrament, every care and attention should be used in preparing the altar bread. It should be easy to break and should not be unpleasant for the

faithful to eat. Bread which tastes of uncooked flour, or which becomes dry and inedible too quickly, must never be used.[14]

Not all the baked products came out that well. Some were hard; others produced extensive crumbs; still others tasted more like cake than bread.

In addition, while the thick, but flat loaves certainly looked unleavened, authorities questioned whether shortening in fact was not a form of yeast, thus rendering the breads leavened and inappropriate.

Finally, these new substantial altar breads required chewing and true eating, not simply swallowing. Because for years most Catholics were taught not to chew the host or even allow it to touch their teeth, this new kind of communion produced an unsettling effect among some.

In the face of these mixed products, controverted recipes and occasional complaints, Vatican authorities saw the need to clarify the situation and did so with these words in the *Norms on Eucharistic Practices:*

> Faithful to Christ's example, the church has constantly used bread and wine mixed with water to celebrate the Lord's Supper. The bread for the celebration of the eucharist, in accordance with the tradition of the whole church, must be made solely of wheat, and, in accordance with the tradition proper to the Latin church, it must be unleavened. By reason of the sign, the matter of the eucharistic celebration "should appear as actual food." This is to be understood as linked to

the consistency of the bread, and not to its form, which remains the traditional one.

No other ingredients are to be added to the wheaten flour and water. The preparation of the bread requires attentive care, to ensure that the product does not detract from the dignity due to the eucharistic bread, can be broken in a dignified way, does not give rise to excessive fragments and does not offend the sensibilities of the faithful when they eat it.[15]

While the most recent directives are clear and precise, there does seem to be a bit of confusion over and conflict between the pattern or ideal presented in the earlier Roman documents and the current norms.

Even within the restrictions noted, however, some religious communities and commercial firms have developed hosts which are somewhat thicker and larger. The celebrant's altar bread, for example, may be 6-8 inches in diameter and can be broken into a few particles for communicants.

• As noted, the hosts reserved should, ideally, have been consecrated at the Mass itself. The church has urged that repeatedly since Vatican II. Nevertheless, a common practice in parishes is to store a large quantity of consecrated breads in the tabernacle and distribute all or most of the hosts from that source.

With minimum effort that situation could be corrected. Since the number of communicants at each Mass weekend after weekend is relatively constant, a count made for a month should give a reasonably accurate estimate of the quantity required. These could be set out for consecration at the particular liturgy every Sunday and would take care of most of the congregation. The few additional ones needed could be taken from the tabernacle and the surplus returned there. The only inconvenience would be minimal extra effort in preparation of ciboria and purification of vessels.

• When the eucharistic assembly is large and communion is to be distributed under both kinds, "it is desirable not to have the additional plates and cups necessary for communion on the altar. A solution is to use one large breadplate and either one large chalice or a large flagon until the breaking of the bread. At the fraction, any other chalices or plates needed are brought to the altar. While the bread is broken on sufficient plates for sharing, the ministers of the cups pour from the flagon into the communion chalices."[16]

• The eucharistic prayer is the center and high point of the celebration. In a dialogue format between celebrant and congregation, it contains these basic elements: thanksgiving (especially in the preface); acclamation (Sanctus), epiclesis (calling forth of the Spirit upon the gifts), institutional narrative and consecration, anamnesis (memorial or remembering), offering, intercessions and final doxology. The people's part is to listen in silent reverence and share in the eucharistic prayer by making the acclamations.

• "Only the eucharistic prayers included in the Roman Missal or those that the Apostolic See has by law admitted . . . are to be used. To modify the eucharistic prayers approved by the church or to adopt others privately composed is a most serious abuse."[17]

At this writing, nine eucharistic prayers have been authorized for the United States: the four found in the sacramentary; three for use with children; two for reconciliation.[18]

We should note that the fourth eucharistic prayer must be employed with its own preface. Consequently, on Sundays or feasts when a unique preface is required (for example, Christmas, Easter, Lent, Advent, Immaculate Conception), this text should not be used.

The United States Bishops' Committee on the Liturgy has made rather extensive observations on this point:

> The use of unauthorized eucharistic prayers and the modification of approved ones are judged to be grave abuses of church discipline. To understand this position a sense of history and an understanding of the ecclesial nature of liturgical prayer are necessary.
>
> The eucharistic prayer traces its origins to the Last Supper table prayer, the berakah over the bread and wine pronounced by Jesus in conformity with Jewish tradition. While using the traditional blessings he gave them a new dimension with the words: "This is my body . . . This is my blood" and "Do this in memory of me."

The early church continued this practice with the presiding minister improvising on the berekah structure with its theme of praise, thanksgiving and supplication. History, however, documents how improvisation of the anaphora moved quickly to fixed texts. In addition to the fact that some celebrants found the task of improvisation too difficult and laborious, greater concern was expressed for the orthodoxy of the prayers. Providing a model prayer of unquestionable orthodoxy, Hippolytus of Rome (3rd century) exhorted the celebrant: "let his prayer be correct and right in doctrine." That same doctrinal concern over worship, and especially the presidential prayer, is operative today. The *lex orandi lex credendi* principle is basic to the church's vigilance over the theological content of all liturgical texts. "The use of unauthorized texts means a loss of the necessary connection between the *lex orandi* and the *lex credendi*."

No one would want to imply that every unauthorized prayer is necessarily doctrinally suspect. Rather, from an ecclesiological perspective it would seem that the Congregation wishes to stress that the eucharistic prayer, by its very nature, must be the prayer of the church, not of an individual. The 1973 Letter to the Presidents of Episcopal Conferences, *Eucharistiae Participationem,* stated: "The ecclesial dimension of the eucharistic prayer should be considerd paramount" (no. 11). The prayer not only is to express the unity of the assembly, but is to be a true profession of faith expressing the nature of the church itself. "Nowhere is this more apparent than in the eucharistic prayer, for there it is not just an individual person, nor even a local community, but 'the one and only Catholic Church, existing in the local churches' that addresses itself to God."[19]

• "Personal modification of approved texts is a phenomenon to be discontinued. Defects in the vernacular translation have led to alterations; alienating vocabulary has encouraged adjustment. While not condoning these personal initiatives, it is hoped that a retranslation of the eucharistic prayers will alleviate the real difficulties – unforeseen when originally prepared in the vernacular translation."[20]

The "alienating vocabulary" phrase apparently refers to instances of so-called sexist language weaknesses, particularly in eucharistic prayer IV.

• The *Newsletter* of the Bishops' Committee on the Liturgy points out that the *Norms on Eucharistic Practices* does "not address a more serious abuse: The position of some Roman Catholics (a small minority in the U.S.A.) who totally reject the new eucharistic prayers, clinging adamantly to the unrevised Roman Canon. This is a most serious error since it calls into question the authority of the pope, the council and the church itself. Here lie the dangerous roots of schism."[21]

• The *Norms on Eucharistic Practices* states, "It is reserved to the priest, by virtue of his ordination, to proclaim the eucharistic prayer which of its nature is the high point of the whole celebration. It is therefore an abuse to have some parts of the eucharistic prayer said by the deacon, by a lower minister or by the faithful."[22]

Along these same lines the BCL *Newsletter* states: "The introduction of the vernacular in the liturgy . . . promoted every member of the assembly to be able to articulate the sacred prayer of thanksgiving. Yet, not only is there no historical precedent for such development but, more importantly, it would contradict the church's constant understanding of the fundamental role of the ordained priest in Christian worship. It is in the person of Christ that the priest offers to the Father the prayer of Christ and those united with him in faith. Precisely as the representative of Christ, in virtue of a sacramental character, and as the head of the faith community, *ex officio,* is the ordained alone empowered to proclaim the eucharistic prayer."[23]

• The deacon invites the people to join in the memorial acclamation, assists in holding the chalice at the "Through him, with him . . ." and encourages all to exchange the sign of peace.

• The assembly or congregation does not remain passive and inert during the eucharistic prayer. "It unites itself to the priest in faith and silence and shows its concurrence by the various interventions provided for in the course of the eucharistic prayer: the responses to the Preface dialogue, the Sanctus, the acclamation after the Consecration, and the final Amen after the Per

Ipsum. The Per Ipsum itself is reserved to the priest. This Amen especially should be emphasized by being sung, since it is the most important in the whole Mass."[24]

The Bishops' Committee on the Liturgy comments: "Three acclamations within the eucharistic prayer merit attention: the Holy, the memorial acclamation, and the great Amen. It is of their nature that they be rhythmically strong, melodically appealing, and affirmative" (*Music in Catholic Worship,* no. 53). Many parishes have implemented the directive of the bishops that these acclamations "ought to be sung, even at Masses in which little else is sung" (*MCW,* no. 54). More attention needs to be given these acclamations in those places where the "four hymn" music format constitutes the sole repertoire and practice. All, finally, are asked to respect the nature of the acclamations and not make them into lengthy pieces of music.[25]

• When the preface is not sung, organ background music during its proclamation can act as a helpful bridge and immediate entrance into the community's singing of the "Holy, holy, holy."

• The American bishops voted to adopt the rubrics governing the congregation's posture so that the people would kneel from after the Sanctus until the completion of the Amen of the eucharistic prayer, that is before the Lord's Prayer.[26]

• Concelebrants should not say the entire

eucharistic prayer together (commonly done with eucharistic prayer II), but only the parts assigned, with the principal celebrant or a single concelebrant taking the other sections. Moreover, their voices should be subdued and not overwhelm the principal celebrant's proclamation. Finally, they should be present from the start and remain until the end.

The congregation should not recite or sing the doxology; its part is a strong, affirming "Amen" in response. At concelebrated Masses, the doxology may be said or sung by the celebrant alone or by all of the concelebrants. If the worshiping congregation is made up totally or almost totally of concelebrants, some or all of them may wish to exercise this option by not joining in the doxology, but by responding with the Amen.

The admonition to concelebrants to use subdued tones and not to overwhelm the celebrant's proclamation is commonly disregarded in the United States. That misconception also interferes with a proper proclamation urged by the following Vatican text.

• "It should be remembered that the eucharistic prayer must not be overlaid with other prayers or songs. When proclaiming the eucharistic prayer, the priest is to pronounce the text clearly so as to make it easy for the faithful to understand it, and so as to foster the formation of a true assembly entirely intent upon the celebration of the memorial of the Lord."[27]

Once again, the BCL *Newsletter* has pertinent observations: "The manner in which the eucharistic prayer is to be proclaimed is the subject of this paragraph. Several points can be developed. First of all, the prayer is addressed to the Father (not the community) but in the name of the entire assembly. However, it should be proclaimed so that it is heard and understood by all present. More specifically, 'When the priest says a prayer, especially a eucharistic prayer, he should not only avoid a dry, monotonous style of delivery, but an overly subjective and emotional way of speaking and acting as well.' The nature of the prayer demands that no other prayers or songs be introduced into, or compete with the proclamation of the eucharistic prayer. This would encompass, for example, both the use of unauthorized acclamations as well as private individual, silent devotional prayers. Furthermore, the prayer is to stand by itself without what might be termed 'mood music' or less felicitously 'Muzak.' In some places the General Instruction directive has been forgotten: 'While the priest is speaking, there should be no other prayer or song, and the organ and other musical instruments should be silent.' "[28]

• The use of bells remains a legitimate option. "A little before the consecration, the minister may ring a bell as a signal to the people. According to local custom, he also rings the bell at each elevation."[29]

• There should be no breaking of the host at the institutional narrative or consecration. Later rubrics explicitly reserve that action for the Lamb of God.

• The celebrant genuflects after each elevation of the consecrated elements; concelebrants bow profoundly.

• During the "Through him, with him . . ." only one chalice and plate are elevated. If there are concelebrants, they do not hold extra cups and ciboria. A deacon or one concelebrant may assist the principal celebrant in this regard by holding the chalice.

• The sign of peace is basically meant to be exchanged among persons next to one another. At parish weekend Masses, the practice of the celebrant coming down from the sanctuary and greeting all those along the center aisle tends to prolong the rite unduly and give a false hierarchical impression. It suggests that this peace of Christ emanates from the altar and moves through the celebrant to the members of the community. The more appropriate manner simply reflects the invitation, "Let us show one another a sign of peace." The celebrant in that approach extends his greeting to those around the altar.

Weekday liturgies with small clusters of people, major feasts like Christmas, and special Masses for children are exceptions at which it seems pastorally effective to have the celebrant or designated persons share the sign of peace with the congregation. In those situations a few words at the invitation are needed to explain this variation.

This gesture of community peace can get a bit out of hand at special group Masses; for example, for Marriage Encounter and Charismatic prayer groups. During these, the Lamb of God, shouted out by the celebrant, becomes something of a rallying cry to restore order and resume the flow of the liturgy.

While the handshake has become common, neither universal nor national legislation has determined a specific form or words, thus leaving it to local development.[30] It might be interesting to note how at the conclusion of the Council of Jerusalem, Paul and Barnabas received the "handclasp of fellowship" from James, Caphas and John (Gal 2:9).

• The Roman Missal explains the meaning and importance behind the *fractio panis* or "breaking of bread" as well as indicating this should occur during the reciting or, better, singing, of the *Agnus Dei*.

"Breaking of bread: this gesture of Christ at the Last Supper gave the entire eucharistic action its name in apostolic times. In addition to its practical aspect, it signifies that in communion we who are many are one body in the one bread of life which is Christ (see I Cor 10:17).

"Agnus Dei: during the breaking of the bread and the commingling, the Agnus Dei is ordinarily sung by the choir or cantor with the people responding; or it may be said aloud. This invocation may be repeated as often as necessary to accompany the breaking of the bread, and is brought to a close by the words, grant us peace."[31]

The celebrant should move on with the breaking and commingling while the people sing or recite the Lamb of God. He should always break at least a few particles from the large host for communicants. The commingling prayer is said quietly by the priest.

• The two prayers before communion, only one of which is used, are meant to be said quietly by the celebrant since they have been designed for the "private preparation of the priest." The faithful also prepare for communion at this time "by praying silently."[32] Similarly, the words, "May the body of Christ bring me . . ." and "May the blood of Christ bring me . . ." are said quietly by the priest.[33]

• Extraordinary ministers of the Eucharist, whether religious or lay, should assist the priests, not replace them for the distribution of communion. "A reprehensible attitude is shown by those priests, who, though present at the celebration, refrain from distributing communion and leave this task to the laity."[34]

• "It is of the greatest importance that the minister avoid all rush and haste. His or her ministration of communion should be done with dignity and reverence."[35] Since the "Amen" said by the faithful is an act of personal faith in the presence of Christ, the minister should give communicants an opportunity to speak that "Amen" before placing the consecrated particle upon their tongue or in their hand.[36] Bad habits and rushed patterns have already developed in which communicants say "Amen" before the minister can even say "The Body of Christ," or ministers distribute the host before communicants can speak their "Amen."

• "With regard to the manner of going to communion, the faithful can receive it either kneeling or standing, in accordance with the norms laid down by the episcopal conference. 'When the faithful communicate kneeling, no other sign of reverence toward the Blessed Sacrament is required, since kneeling is itself a sign of adoration. When they receive communion standing, it is strongly recommended that, coming up in procession, they should make a sign of reverence before receiving the sacrament. This should be done at the right time and place, so that the order of people going to and from communion is not disrupted.' "[37]

The kind of gesture urged here is not clear. However, American Catholics already have customs which seem to reflect that external act of reverence and adoration: folded hands, a sign of the cross just before or after receiving the host, crossed arms when receiving on the tongue, or a simple bow. After receiving in the hand, it can involve stepping aside, stopping, gazing at the host for a moment of adoration, placing the particle in the mouth and then returning to one's seat.

Communicants should not pick up the consecrated bread and the sacred chalice; nor should they hand them from one to another. Communion is a gift from the Lord, given to the faithful through the minister appointed for this purpose.[38] Still, the most practical, safe and reverent way of distributing communion from the chalice is for the minister to hand the cup totally to the recipient, and then take it back and extend it to the next communicant, rather than tipping the vessel toward the person.

• "It is most desirable that the faithful should receive the body of the Lord in hosts consecrated at the same Mass and should share the cup when it is permitted."[39]

"The sign of communion is more complete when given under both kinds, since in that form the sign of the eucharistic meal appears more clearly."[40]

"To eat and drink is of the essence of the symbolic fullness of this sacrament. Communion under one kind is an example of minimizing of primary symbols."[41]

That desirable, more complete, fuller procedure of communion under both kinds has spread rapidly and with spiritual success in the United States. The officially permitted occasions have multiplied until in 1978 the American bishops authorized it on Sundays when pastorally feasible and beneficial in a local situation.

Since that extension, many parishes in our own diocese have implemented this with ease at all weekend liturgies. The difficulties have been few; the objections almost non-existent, since it always remains an option; the number of persons choosing the cup between 50-75 per cent.

To insure, as the *Norms on Eucharistic Practices* insists, "the reverence due to the sacrament," and "the good of those receiving the Eucharist," parish leaders need to have ample ministers (two cup ministers for every one distributing the hosts), clean linens and suitable vessels. There should be a precise delineation of duties for the distributors, a clear and adequate explanation to the congregation, and procession procedures that provide easy, free alternatives for each person.

Only in this way can a Sunday congregation be termed "clearly defined, well disciplined and homogeneous."[42] However, the American genius for dealing with large numbers in an efficient manner appears to have made that possible.

• The "consecrated wine is to be consumed immediately after communion and may not be kept. Care must be taken to consecrate only the amount of wine needed for communion."[43] As with the number of hosts, some experience in a parish will determine fairly accurately the quantity of wine required. If, however, an occasional misjudgment occurs and the amount remaining is larger than can be prudently consumed by ministers and others, it would seem appropriate to store the surplus in the tabernacle for use at the next Mass.

We have a legal precedent for such a recommendation. Article 95 for the *Rite of Anointing and Pastoral Care of the Sick* states: "If Mass is not celebrated in the presence of the sick person, the blood of the Lord should be kept in a properly covered chalice which is placed in the tabernacle after Mass." That rubric still holds force and would not be cancelled out by the directive of the General Instruction.

• The communion vessels may be purified after Mass at a side table or presumably in the sacristy near the sacrarium, especially if there are several of them. There are good reasons to recommend this procedure at weekend or other liturgies.[44]

• What was said about the entrance antiphon when there is no singing also applies to the communion verse.

The General Instruction states: "If there is no singing, the antiphon in the Missal is recited either by the people, by some of them, or by a reader. Otherwise the priest himself says it after he receives communion and before he gives communion to the congregation."[45]

The American Foreword, however, comments: "The communion antiphon, although it is not ordinarily to be said by the priest, has also been included for completeness. . . . For use of the communion antiphon if there is no singing, the above commentary on the entrance antiphon is applicable."[46]

In the Entrance Antiphon section, to repeat, the American bishops mentioned that these antiphons are printed in smaller type to indicate they are not ordinarily said by the priest and are not parts of a sacramentary.

Moreover, the Roman Missal presumes there

will be singing at such processions like communion. If psalms with antiphons are not employed other permitted songs will be substituted.

Perhaps the best way to resolve the difficulty when there is no singing at communion is for the celebrant or another person prior to distribution of the eucharist to read the antiphon with an invitation for participants to use this as a point or theme of reflection.

• The *Norms* urge the faithful to make a proper thanksgiving after communion. They may do this during the celebration with a period of silence, a hymn, a psalm or other song of praise. After the celebration they may do this by staying behind to pray for a suitable time.[47] Even if there is a song during the celebration, it is desirable to have a pause for silent reflection.

• Following communion, the altar should be cleared by the server who takes the sacramentary to the chair for use at the concluding prayer.

The announcements, which should be brief, ought to be made following the prayer after communion.

The Mass swiftly concludes. Nourished by the word of God and the bread of life, the community is now ready to be sent forth carrying the Good News to others.

Chapter Seven:

Concluding Rite

The concluding rite consists of:

a) the priest's greeting and blessing which is on certain days and occasions expanded by the prayer over the people or other solemn form;

b) the dismissal which sends each member of the congregation to do good works, praising and blessing the Lord.

The Roman Missal, General Instruction[1]

• As we noted in the last chapter, any brief announcements are to be made following the prayer after communion.[2]

The announcements should be short, not a repetition of all the bulletin details. Parishioners will swiftly stop reading the weekly handout, if they know the identical announcements are made at Mass. Normally only a few major concerns ought to be noted and sometimes none will require mention during the liturgy. This approach both enhances the worship and also increases interest in the bulletin which ushers distribute, ideally, as the people leave the church.

Making the announcements while the people stand leaves something to be desired and having the congregation sit for them is even less desirable. In the one case, interest or attention seems low because of the standing posture. A sense of anxiousness to leave appears to pervade the community, making members restless and able only to half-hear the announcements. For the congregation to be seated again, after standing for a brief prayer, creates an unsatisfactory jack-in-the-box effect.

Minimal announcements can best resolve that tension. On those truly rare occasions when a longer presentation is needed, e.g., at an ordination, confirmation or similar major event in the parish, the people could be seated for the remarks of acknowledgment or gratitude normally offered at such celebrations.

Since the purpose of the concluding rite and dismissal is to send each member of the congregation out to do good works, praising and blessing the Lord, the celebrant might wish at this time to summarize in two or three sentences the theme and practical import of the day's homily. Such a mini-homily would recall the overall thrust of the day's liturgy, lead naturally into the needed announcements and dismiss participants with a sharper awareness of how they specifically will be seeking to do good works in the week ahead.

• The expanded solemn blessing or prayer over the people begins with the celebrant's, "The Lord be with you," continues with an invitation by the priest or deacon, "Bow your heads and pray for God's blessing," and concludes with the multiple blessing or prayer.

Experience indicates that proper inflection, sufficient pauses and even an occasional reminder of the desired response are needed to have the community offer a significant "Amen" after each versicle.

• "If a liturgical service follows the Mass, the concluding rite (greeting, blessing, and dismissal) is omitted."[3] This occurs particularly at funerals. In those circumstances the celebrant completes the prayer after communion, then, without further words, kisses the altar, and moves to the proper place for the commendation rite.

• Ordinarily the priest kisses the altar before leaving the sanctuary.[4]

• For the celebrant to process down one of the main aisles and remain at the entrance to greet parishioners is far superior to his disappearing into the sacristy, isolated from the community.

I would like to note with commentary here a few other points from the *Norms on Eucharistic Practices.*

• Purification of the vessels following communion may be done by persons other than the celebrant. These include the special eucharistic ministers. However, they ought to carry out this cleansing at the side table, not at the altar, and preferably after Mass. There are several reasons for that suggestion: with the altar facing the people, the purification before everyone seems inappropriate; by postponing the cleansing, more time can be spent by all in silence and the optional song of praise; in large celebrations or when communion is given under both kinds, the washing of all vessels unduly delays the rite itself.[5]

"Use is not to be made of simple baskets or other recipients meant for ordinary use outside the sacred celebrations, nor are the sacred vessels to be of poor quality or lacking any artistic style.

"Before being used, chalices and patens must be blessed by the bishop or by a priest."[6]

A simple revised rite for this blessing can be found in Chapter VII of the text *Dedication of a Church and an Altar.*

The American bishops have approved other materials besides gold or silver for these altar chalices and vessels, provided they meet the standards indicated in various decrees. Thus ceramic and wood creations would be satisfactory, if they are functionally appropriate and measure up to the quality demanded.

"Like the plates and chalices or flagons, all other vessels and implements used in the liturgical celebration should be of such quality and design that they speak of the importance of the ritual action."[7]

• The period of prayer and reflection recommended after communion should emphasize the notion of praise.

> The so-called litany or prayer of thanksgiving, occasionally introduced after communion, even at the expense of the silent period, is inappropriate and a distortion of the eucharistic (thanksgiving) ritual. It has been correctly noted that even the prayer after communion is not a prayer of thanksgiving (as onetime thought) but a final petition that what has been celebrated might be put into daily practice.
>
> Without denying that the communicant is both grateful and humble for the great gift received, the proper sentiment at this moment in the rite is *praise.* It is the twofold eucharistic theme of praise and thanksgiving which is properly continued throughout the day in both personal and communal prayer (e.g. in the celebration of the Liturgy of the Hours).[8]

This moment of silent reflection and praise of God following communion is distinct from the desirable period after the liturgy which is still called the *Gratiarum actio post Missam* or thanksgiving after Mass. The time after communion is a communal action of silence and/or song (including silence even when there is song); the moments after Mass normally take on a more individualized character.

• The *Norms* mention the role of women in the liturgy, but add without explanation that they "are not however permitted to act as altar servers."[9]

While this restriction has been painful for some to accept, the Bishops' Committee on the Liturgy points out that in comparison to the many other roles now open for women the server's function is relatively insignificant.

> The role of women in the liturgy is already extensive. They may proclaim the sacred scriptures from the same ambo as the bishop, priest, and deacon. They can participate in liturgical processions (e.g. presentation of the gifts). They may be properly authorized to handle the sacred bread and wine as special ministers of the eucharist within and outside the Mass. They may assist the community in music as leader of song, cantor, psalmist, organist, choir member. They may be authorized to lead a communion service when no priest or deacon is available. They can, with permission, expose the blessed sacrament. They may serve as commentators and place the important intentions of prayer before the entire community in the General Intercessions. They can minister hospitality as ushers.[10]

• Home Masses should follow the guidelines of the 1969 *Instruction on Masses for Special Groups* which require, among other elements, that the bishop give permission and they not be celebrated on Sundays or holy days of obligation.[11]

The reasons for that restriction are the unity of the parish community and the preeminent importance of the Sunday or holy day liturgies in the life of the worshiping community. Small or particular group Masses on the Lord's Day held in churches or chapels and, even more, held in private homes, tend to split that parish unit, diminish the power of the Sunday liturgy and encourage a certain elitism. Such desirable home celebrations are better arranged for weekdays. If a special group needs to assemble for the Eucharist on Sunday, this could be integrated into the parish liturgy.

• "Public and private devotion to the Holy Eucharist outside Mass also is highly recommended: for the presence of Christ, who is adored by the faithful in the sacrament, derives from the sacrifice and is directed towards sacramental and spiritual communion."[12]

We mentioned earlier the 1973 section of the revised Roman Ritual entitled *Holy Communion and Worship of the Eucharist Outside of Mass* which clarifies the proper relationship between the Mass and eucharistic devotions. The elimination of the double genuflection and the reduction of candles were noted as two practical reform measures designed to underscore this proper balance.

A rereading of this document and consideration of current American practices will show how certain contrary procedures need to be updated. The Bishops' Committee on the Liturgy has summarized both those practices and the pertinent references on the document:

> 1) During exposition of the blessed sacrament, the celebration of Mass is prohibited in the body of the church (no. 83). 2) Eucharistic devotions

must be prepared in harmony with the liturgy and the liturgical year (no. 90). 3) The directives for the revised rite (nos. 82-112) must be followed in the exposition of the holy eucharist and benediction. 4) Exposition which is held exclusively for the giving of benediction is prohibited (no. 89). 5) During the exposition there should be prayers, songs, and readings to direct the attention of the faithful to the worship of Christ the Lord (no. 95).[13]

• "The tabernacle in which the Eucharist is kept can be located on an altar, or away from it, in a spot in the church which is very prominent, truly noble and duly decorated, or in a chapel suitable for private prayer and for adoration by the faithful."[14]

In the 1967 *Instruction on the Worship of the Eucharistic Mystery,* section 55 noted that during the celebration of Mass the principal modes of worship by which Christ is present to his church are gradually revealed. "First of all, Christ is seen to be present among the faithful gathered in his name; then in his Word, as the Scriptures are read and explained; in the person of the minister; finally and in a unique way (*modo singulari*) under the species of the Eucharist."

As a practical conclusion to this with regard to the placement of the tabernacle, it goes on: "Consequently, by reason of the symbolism, it is more in keeping with the nature of the celebration that the eucharistic presence of Christ, which is the fruit of the consecration and should be seen as such, should not be on the altar from the very beginning of Mass through the reservation of the sacred species in the tabernacle."

Thus the Eucharist is best kept in a place distinct from the altar and place of celebration.

The *Newsletter* of the Bishops' Committee on the Liturgy has some helpful clarifications about the tabernacle veil:

> Traditionally the tabernacle was covered with a veil, a *conopaeum,* which helped to symbolize the tabernaculum-tent of the Old Testament and recall the mystery of the incarnation in which "the Word was made flesh and pitched his *tent* among us" (John 1:14). It was a sign, furthermore, of the reservation. With new designs for tabernacles, seldom any longer cast in the dome or pyramidal shape, yet dignified and properly ornamented, which one hesitates to cover up, the use of the tabernacle veil is no longer universal or insisted upon in the dioceses of the U.S.A. by the competent authority. Although the veil is no longer the certain sign of the presence of the blessed sacrament in the tabernacle in many churches, the sanctuary lamp has become so. As a matter of practice, in the U.S.A., the lamp has become a sign of presence more than a sign of honor toward the reserved eucharist.[15]

• "The venerable practice of genuflecting before the Blessed Sacrament, whether enclosed in the tabernacle or publicly exposed, as a sign of adoration, is to be maintained. This act requires that it be performed in a recollected way. In order that the heart may bow before God in profound reverence, the genuflection must be neither hurried nor careless."[16]

That last sentence capsulizes in a practical directive what both this book and true worship are all about.

Liturgy involves the whole person, the inner and outer self, body and spirit. It does necessarily include rubrics, which concentrate mainly on external objects and actions, but moves beyond those visible elements and incorporates the heart as well.

Just as a careful genuflection can aid the heart in bowing reverently before God, so, too, liturgical ministers who take serious pains to follow the official rubrics will help themselves and those they serve lift their spirits to the Lord above.

Pure rubrical worship without the heart becomes lifeless and debilitating. Liturgy without proper rubrics becomes chaotic and confusing. Combined in a proper balance they lift up the total individual, body, soul and spirit, and the entire community in praise of the awesome God, yet loving Father.

Footnotes

Part I:
The Past and Future Decades

Chapter One: Ten Years of Progress

1. Champlin, Joseph. *Christ Present and Yet to Come.* Maryknoll: Orbis Books, 1971.

2. *Documents of Vatican II.* Walter M. Abbott, S.J., General Editor. New York: The American Press, 1966. *Constitution on the Sacred Liturgy,* article 30.

3. *General Instruction of the Roman Missal.* Translated by International Committee on English in the Liturgy, Inc. Toronto, Canada, 1969, article 313.

4. *Documents of Vatican II, op. cit.,* article 11.

5. *Norms on Eucharistic Practices.* Rome: Congregation for the Sacraments and Divine Worship, April 17, 1980. "Translation issued by the Vatican." Foreword, paragraph 3.

6. *Vatican Council II.* Austin Flannery, O.P., General Editor. Northport, N.Y.: Costello Publishing Company. *Constitution on the Sacred Liturgy,* article 35.

7. *Ibid.*, article 51.

8. *Ibid.*, article 27.

9. *Vatican Council II, op. cit., Pastoral Constitution on the Church in the Modern World,* article 1.

10. *General Instruction of the Roman Missal, op. cit.,* article 45.

11. Gallen, John, S.J. "Reforming the Liturgy, Again." *America,* November 22, 1980, p. 324.

Chapter Two: A Little Too Far and Too Fast?

1. *Vatican Council II, op. cit., Constitution on the Sacred Liturgy,* article 22.

2. *Ibid.*, article 21.

3. *Ibid.*, article 23.

4. *Norms on Eucharistic Practices, op. cit.,* Foreword, paragraph 4.

5. *Vatican Council II, op. cit.,* article 30.

6. *Norms on Eucharistic Practices, op. cit.,* paragraph 4.

7. *Ibid.*, paragraph 10.

8. *Ibid.*, Foreword, paragraph 4.

9. O'Rourke, David K., O.P. "Eggheads, Pumpkin Heads and Liturgical Popularism." *Commonweal,* April 25, 1980, pp. 234-237.

10. Garvey, John, "Somebody Stole the Mass." *Notre Dame Magazine,* July, 1980.

11. *Norms on Eucharistic Practices, op. cit.,* Foreword, paragraph 4.

12. Garvey, John, *op. cit.*, p. 23.

13. *Norms on Eucharistic Practices, op. cit.,* Foreword, paragraph 8.

14. Toffler, Alvin, *Future Shock.* New York: Random House, 1970, p. 5.

15. *Ibid.,* pp. 297-300.

Chapter Three: A Proper Balance

1. Wood, Kenneth. "Awe—An Essential of Worship." *Ministry,* November, 1980, pp. 13-14.

2. Pope John Paul II. *Mystery and Worship of the Holy Eucharist,* 1980 Holy Thursday letter for all the bishops of the church. English translation from the Vatican as it appears in *Origins,* March 27, 1980, Volume 9: No. 41, pp. 658-659.

3. *General Instruction of the Roman Missal, op. cit.,* article 23.

4. Psalm 99, verses 1-3, from Morning Prayer, Week III, *The Liturgy of the Hours.* New York: Catholic Book Publishing Company, 1975, Volume I, Advent/Christmas Season.

5. Wood, Kenneth, *op. cit.,* p. 14.

6. Dulles, Avery, S.J. *Models of the Church.* Garden City, N.Y.: Doubleday and Company, Inc., 1974, p. 18.

7. *Environment and Art in Catholic Worship.* Published, 1978, by the U.S. Bishops' Committee on the Liturgy and Federation of Diocesan Liturgical Commissions. Articles 1, 2. The text appears in *The Liturgy Documents: A Parish Resource.* Chicago: Liturgy Training Program, 1980, p. 216.

8. *Ibid.,* article 14, p. 219

9. *Ibid.,* article 15, p. 219.

10. *Instruction and Liturgical Formation in Seminaries,* Sacred Congregation for Catholic Education, June 3, 1979, article 58.

11. *Ibid.,* article 20.

12. Acts 2: 42-47 (NAB).

13. *Vatican Council II, op. cit. Constitution on the Sacred Liturgy,* article 26.

14. Pope John Paul II, *op. cit.,* article 4, p. 656.

15. *Norms on Eucharistic Practices, op. cit.,* paragraph 27.

Part II:
The Mass: A Review for Liturgical Ministers and Leaders

Chapter Four: Introductory Rites

1. *General Instruction of the Roman Missal, op. cit.,* article 24.

2. *Ibid.,* articles 82, 84, 270. *Environment and Art in Catholic Worship, op. cit.,* articles 86, 88.

3. *Ibid.,* articles 79, 84, 269. *Environment and Art in Catholic Worship, op. cit.,* articles 89. *Holy Communion and Worship of the Eucharist Outside Mass,* article 85, as it appears in *The Rites of the Catholic Church.* New York: Pueblo Publishing Company, 1976, pp. 486-487.

4. *Environment and Art in Catholic Worship, op. cit.,* article 91.

5. *Ibid.,* article 92.

6. *General Instruction of the Roman Missal, op. cit.,* article 80.

7. *Environment and Art in Catholic Worship,* article 103.

8. For some detailed suggestions, cf. Champlin, Joseph. *An Important Office of Immense Love: A Handbook for Eucharistic Ministers.* New York: Paulist Press, 1980, pp. 118-138.

9. *General Instruction of the Roman Missal, op. cit.,* article 25.

10. *Ibid.,* article 26.

11. Foreword to the *General Instruction of the Roman Missal, op. cit.,* no. 18, p. 76.

12. *General Instruction of the Roman Missal, op. cit.,* article 30.

13. *Music in Catholic Worship,* published by the United States Bishops' Committee on the Liturgy, November, 1967. The text appears in *The Liturgy Documents, op. cit.,* article 65.

14. *Vatican Council II, op. cit., Constitution on the Sacred Liturgy,* article 34.

15. *General Instruction of the Roman Missal, op. cit.,* article 32.

16. Foreword to the *General Instruction of the Roman Missal, op. cit.,* no. 11, p. 71.

Chapter Five: Liturgy of the Word

1. *General Instruction of the Roman Missal, op. cit.,* article 33.

2. *Newsletter,* Bishops' Committee on the Liturgy, Washington: Volume XVI, August-September, 1980, p. 223.

3. *Directory for Masses with Children,* 1973, as it appears in *The Liturgy Documents: A Parish Resource, op. cit.,* article 42, p. 183.

4. *Norms on Eucharistic Practices, op. cit.,* paragraph 1.

5. *Newsletter, op. cit.,* p. 224.

6. Pope John Paul II. *Mystery and Worship of the Holy Eucharist, op. cit.,* no. 10.

7. *Norms on Eucharistic Practices, op. cit.,* paragraph 2.

8. Walsh, Eugene A., S.S. *Practical Suggestions for Celebrating Sunday Mass.* Old Hickory, Tennessee: Pastoral Arts Association of North America, 1978, pp. 51-52.

9. *Lectionary of Sunday Readings,* for A, B or C Cycle, Pueblo Publishing Company, 1860 Broadway, New York, N.Y. 10023.

10. *Newsletter, op. cit.,* p. 225.

11. *General Instruction of the Roman Missal, op. cit.,* article 39.

12. Walsh, Eugene A., S.S. *The Order of Mass: Guidelines.* Old Hickory, Tennessee: Pastoral Arts Association of North America, 1979, p. 33.

13. *Newsletter, op. cit.,* p. 224.

14. *Norms on Eucharistic Practices, op. cit.,* paragraph 3.

15. *Newsletter, op. cit.,* p. 225.

16. *General Instruction of the Roman Missal, op. cit.,* article 95.

17. *Ibid.,* article 95.

18. *Ibid.,* article 97.

19. *Ibid.,* article 98.

20. *Norms on Eucharistic Practices, op. cit.,* paragraph 1.

Chapter Six: Liturgy of the Eucharist

1. *General Instruction of the Roman Missal, op. cit.,* article 48.

2. *Ibid.,* article 49, 101.

3. *Ibid.*

4. *Ibid.*

5. *Ibid.,* article 50.

6. *Music in Catholic Worship, op. cit.,* article 71.

7. *General Instruction of the Roman Missal, op. cit.,* 49, 50, 54, 55.

8. *Ibid.,* articles 51, 235.

9. *Ibid.,* 102, 103.

10. *Ibid.,* 103, 104, 106.

11. *Ibid.,* 103.

12. *Ibid.,* 107.

13. *Ibid.,* 283.

14. *Vatican Council II, op. cit., Third Instruction on the Correct Implementation of the Constitution on the Sacred Liturgy,* article 5, p. 216.

15. *Norms on Eucharistic Practices, op. cit.,* paragraph 8.

16. *Environment and Art in Catholic Worship, op. cit.,* article 96.

17. *Norms on Eucharistic Practices, op. cit.,* paragraph 5.

18. *Newsletter, op. cit.,* Volume XVI, October, 1980, p. 231.

19. *Ibid.,* pp. 230-231.

20. *Ibid.,* p. 231.

21. *Ibid.,* p. 231.

22. *Norms on Eucharistic Practices, op. cit.,* paragraph 4.

23. *Newsletter, op. cit.,* pp. 229-230.

24. *Norms on Eucharistic Practices, op. cit.,* paragraph 4.

25. *Newsletter, op. cit.,* p. 230.

26. Appendix to the *General Instruction of the Roman Missal, op. cit.,* article 26, p. 152.

27. *Norms on Eucharistic Practices, op. cit.,* paragraph 6.

28. *Newsletter, op. cit.,* p. 231.

29. *General Instruction of the Roman Missal, op. cit.,* article 109.

30. *Ibid.,* article 56 b. See Appendix also.

31. *General Instruction of the Roman Missal, op. cit.,* article 56 c, e.

32. *Ibid.,* article 56 f.

33. *Ibid.,* article 116.

34. *Norms on Eucharistic Practices, op. cit.,* paragraph 10.

35. *Study Text* I, *Holy Communion.* Bishops' Committee on the Liturgy, Washington, D.C.: United States Catholic Conference, 1973, p. 15.

36. *Norms on Eucharistic Practices, op. cit.,* paragraph 11.

37. *Ibid.,* paragraph 11.

38. *Ibid.,* paragraph 9.

39. *General Instruction of the Roman Missal, op. cit.,* article 56 h.

40. *Ibid.,* article 240.

41. *Environment and Art in Catholic Worship, op. cit.,* article 96.

42. *Norms on Eucharistic Practices, op. cit.,* paragraph 12.

43. *Ibid.,* paragraph 14.

44. *General Instruction of the Roman Missal, op. cit.,* article 120.

45. *Ibid.,* article 56 f.

46. Foreword to the *General Instruction of the Roman Missal, op. cit.,* no. 19, p. 76.

47. *Norms on Eucharistic Practices, op. cit.,* paragraph 17.

Chapter Seven: Concluding Rites

1. *General Instruction of the Roman Missal, op. cit.,* article 57.

2. *Ibid.,* article 123.

3. *Ibid.,* article 126.

4. *Ibid.,* article 125.

5. *Newsletter, op. cit.,* 1981.

6. *Norms on Eucharistic Practices, op. cit.,* paragraph 16.

7. *Environment and Art in Catholic Worship, op. cit.,* article 96.

8. *Newsletter, op. cit.,* 1981.

9. *Norms on Eucharistic Practices, op. cit.,* paragraph 18.

10. *Newsletter, op. cit.,* 1981.

11. *Vatican Council II, op. cit., Instruction on Masses for Special Groups,* articles 3, 4, 10, pp. 142-147.

12. *Norms on Eucharistic Practices, op. cit.,* paragraph 20.

13. *Newsletter, op. cit.,* 1981.

14. *Norms on Eucharistic Practices, op. cit.,* paragraphs 24-25.

15. *Newsletter, op. cit.,* 1981.

16. *Norms on Eucharistic Practices, op. cit.,* paragraph 26.